MORE'S *Utopia*

harper 🔥 torchbooks

A reference-list of Harper Torchbooks, classified by subjects, is printed at the end of this volume.

MORE'S *Utopia*

THE BIOGRAPHY OF AN IDEA

BY J. H. HEXTER

Harper Torchbooks · The Academy Library
HARPER & ROW, PUBLISHERS
NEW YORK, EVANSTON, AND LONDON

To the members of
The Columbia University Seminar
on the Renaissance,
Spring 1950

MORE'S UTOPIA

Printed in the United States of America.
This book was originally published in 1952 by
Princeton University Press. It is here reprinted
by arrangement.
First HARPER TORCHBOOK edition published 1965 by
Harper & Row, Publishers, Incorporated
49 East 33rd Street
New York, New York 10016
Library of Congress catalog card number: 52-5843

Contents

CONTENTS

Preface

THIS essay on More's *Utopia* will appear without one of the conventional insignia of the work of scholarship—the bibliography. For the study of More and his best-known book several excellent bibliographical aids are available. Anyone who wishes to pursue further any of the matters dealt with in the following essay will find abundant guidance in R. W. Chambers', *Sir Thomas More,* in Russell Ames', *Citizen Thomas More*, in H. W. Donner's *Introduction to Utopia,* and in Frederick L. Baumann, "Sir Thomas More," a review article in the *Journal of Modern History,* 4, 604-615. In *Moreana 1478-1945* Frank and M. P. Sullivan have published the titles of practically all books and articles centering on More, printed in the past four hundred years. To add to the above list another less complete bibliography in a work in which, with few exceptions, only the most obvious sources and secondary works were used would be a rather ostentatious waste of the reader's time and the publisher's paper.

The appearance of this essay provides me with my first adequate opportunity to make a partial payment on a debt of gratitude that I will never be able fully to repay. Not a single word of the essay was written, its idea was not conceived, during the two years of study that grants from the John Simon Guggenheim Memorial Foundation made possible for me. But without those years of free and undisturbed study which allowed me completely to reorient the direction of my interest in history, I could never have written what follows. Indeed, so much do I owe to the Foundation and to the enlightened policy of its Secretary General, Henry Allen Moe, that whatever competent work I may do in any field of intellectual effort for the rest of my life will in a large measure be due to the splendid opportunity they offered me.

I am also obliged to Dr. Russell Ames, formerly of Queens College, on whom I tried out my earliest sketch of my study of *Utopia,* to Prof. E. H. Harbison of Princeton who read and made invaluable criticisms of the first draft, and to Prof. Garrett Mattingly of Columbia whose encouraging letter to me after he read the second draft will always be one of my most cherished and happy memories. I have also benefited from readings of the manuscript by Profs. George Parks, Koppel Pinson, and Oscar Shaftel of Queens College. In the matter of this book and in all other things I owe more than I can express to my wife. Besides caring for four small children she has in the past months done most of the nasty jobs that inhere in the publication of a book, checking the footnotes, typing up the clean copy, reading proof. Moreover, her excellent ear for inappropriate purple patches has forced me, if not to eliminate them, at least to tone them down to a relatively innocuous lavender.

This essay began as an even more modest project for a paper to be read in the Columbia University Seminar on the Renaissance in the spring of 1950, and to the members of that seminar, to whom it is dedicated, the essay owes most. The advantage of having one's favorite mistakes and illusions firmly knocked over the head in the relative privacy of the Paterno Library by critics at once profoundly learned, altogether friendly, fair, and well disposed, and entirely ruthless is immeasurable. If they helped me eliminate much that was worst in my work, my colleagues also offered me insights that, developed to the best of my limited ability, have become, I believe, among the more adequate parts of the book as it now stands.

Queens College of the City of New York
December 7, 1951

NOTE ON FOOTNOTE CITATIONS*

Since three editions of More's *Utopia*, the Erasmus epistles and their English translations are repeatedly cited in the footnotes of the following essay, I have adopted an abbreviated method of annotation for them:

Sir Thomas More, *Utopia*, ed. J. H. Lupton, cited as L
Sir Thomas More, *Utopia*, Everyman's Library, cited as E
Sir Thomas More, *Utopia*, Clarendon Press, ed. J. C. Collins, cited as C

The numeral in each case indicates the *page* of the indicated edition. Example: L 126, E 51, C 53.

Desiderius Erasmus, *Opus Epistolarum* . . . , ed. P. S. and H. M. Allen, cited as A
Desiderius Erasmus, *Epistles* . . . , ed. and tr. F. M. Nichols, cited as N

The numerals in the Nichols edition indicate volume and *page*, in the Allen edition volume and *number* of the letter, followed by the numbers of the lines. Example: N 2:381; A 2:461, line 1.

The Rogers' edition of More's correspondence is cited as Rogers, followed by the *number* of the letter, and the numbers of the lines.

* See next page for correction of this Note.

Note to the Torchbook edition

The note on page ix was unfortunately out of date at the moment it was being printed, since at that time the Everyman Library had in press a revised edition of *Utopia* with pagination entirely different from the original edition here used. The citations beginning E therefore are of use only to those to whom the original Everyman edition of *Utopia* is available. In order to make easier reference from the Lupton edition of *Utopia* to the *Utopia* volume recently published in the Yale edition of *The Selected Works of St. Thomas More* and to the *Utopia* volume shortly to be published in the Yale edition of the Complete Works of St. Thomas More a collation of the pagination in those three editions follows.

Utopia— Book I

L.	*Y.S.*	*Y.C.*	*L.*	*Y.S.*	*Y.C.*	*L.*	*Y.S.*	*Y.C.*
lxxx		5	xcv		21	10	7	
lxxxi		5	xcvi		21	11	8	
lxxxii		5	xcvii		23	12	8	
lxxxiii		7	xcviii		23	21	9	47
lxxxiv		7	xcix		25	21	9	
lxxxv		9	c		25	22	10	
lxxxvi		9	1	3	39	23	11	
lxxxvii		11	2	3		24	11	49
lxxxviii		11	3	4		25	11	
lxxxix		13	4	4	41	26	12	
xc		13	5	5		27	13	51
xci		15	6	5		28	13	
xcii		15	7	6	43	29	13	
xciii		21	8	6		30	14	53
xciv		19	9	7	45	31	14	

L. = Lupton
Y.S. = Yale Edition of *The Selected Works of St. Thomas More*
Y.C. = Yale Edition of *The Complete Works of St. Thomas More.*

L.	*Y.S.*	*Y.C.*
32	15	
33	15	53
34	16	
35	16	
36	17	57
37	17	
38	18	
39	18	59
40	19	
41	19	
42	20	61
43	20	
44	21	
45	21	63
46	22	
47	22	
48	23	65
49	23	
50	24	
51	24	67
52	25	
53	25	
54	26	69
55	26	
56	27	
57	27	71
58	28	
59	28	
60	29	73
61	29	
62	30	75
63	30	
64	31	
65	31	75
66	32	77
67	32	
68	33	79
69	33	
70	34	
71	34	81
72	35	
73	35	
74	36	83
75	36	
76	37	85
77	38	
78	38	
79	39	87
80	39	
81	40	89
82	41	
83	41	
84	41	
85	42	91
86	42	
87	43	
88	44	93
89	44	
90	45	
91	45	95
92	46	
93	46	
94	47	97
L.	*Y.S.*	*Y.C.*
95	47	
96	48	
97	48	99
98	49	
99	50	
100	50	101
101	51	
102	51	103
103	52	
104	52	
105	53	
106	53	105
107	53	
108	54	
109	54	107
110	55	
111	55	109
112	56	
113	56	
114	57	109

Book 2

L.	*Y.S.*	*Y.C.*
115	59	111
116	59	
117	60	
118	60	113
119	61	
120	61	115
121	62	
122	62	
123	63	117
124	63	
125	63	
126	63	
127	64	119
128	65	
129	65	119
130	65	121
131	66	
132	66	

L.	*Y.S.*	*Y.C.*
133	66	123
134	66	
136	67	
136	67	
137	68	125
138	68	
139	69	
140	69	127
141	70	
142	70	
143	71	129
144	71	
145	72	131
146	72	
147	73	
148	73	133
149	74	
150	74	135
151	75	
152	75	
153	76	
154	76	137
155	76	
156	77	
157	77	139
158	78	
159	78	141
160	79	
161	79	
162	80	143
163	80	
164	81	145
165	81	
166	81	
167	82	147
168	82	

L.	*Y.S.*	*Y.C.*
169	83	
170	83	149
171	84	
172	84	
173	85	
174	85	
175	86	153
176	86	
177	87	
178	87	155
179	87	
180	88	157
181	88	
182	89	
183	90	159
184	90	
185	91	
186	91	161
187	91	
188	92	163
189	92	
190	93	
191	93	165
192	94	
193	94	
194	95	167
195	95	
196	96	169
197	96	
198	97	171
199	97	
200	98	
201	98	
202	99	173
203	99	
204	100	175
205	100	
206	100	
207	101	177
208	101	
209	102	
210	102	179
211	103	
212	103	181
213	104	
214	104	
215	105	
216	105	183
217	106	
218	106	
219	107	185
220	107	
221	108	
222	108	187
223	109	
224	109	
225	110	189

L.	*Y.S.*	*Y.C.*
226	110	
227	111	
228	111	191
229	112	
230	112	
231	113	193
232	113	
233	114	195
234	114	
235	115	
236	115	197
237	116	
238	116	
239	117	199
240	117	

L.	*Y.S.*	*Y.C.*
241	118	
242	118	
243	118	201
244	119	
245	119	
246	120	203
247	120	
248	121	205
249	121	
250	122	
251	122	207
252	123	
253	123	
254	124	209
255	124	
256	125	
257	125	211
258	126	
259	126	213
260	127	
261	128	
262	128	215
263	129	
264	129	
265	129	217
266	130	
267	130	
268	131	219
269	132	
270	132	
271	133	221
272	134	
273	134	
274	134	
275	135	223
276	136	
277	136	
278	137	225
279	137	
280	138	
281	138	227
282	139	
283	139	
284	140	229
285	140	
286	141	
287	141	231
288	142	
289	142	
290	142	233
291	143	
292	143	
293	144	235
294	144	
295	145	237
296	145	
297	145	
298	146	
299	147	239
300	147	
301	148	241
302	148	
303	148	
304	149	243
305	150	
306	150	245
307	151	
308	152	
309	152	247

MORE'S *UTOPIA*:

THE BIOGRAPHY OF AN IDEA

For the Reader: The Idea and the Book

As its title hints, the essay which follows is not the history but the biographical sketch of an idea, the idea for the book called *Utopia*. Like all ideas for books it was born and had its whole life span in the mind of an author. Like all such ideas it ceased to be when the printed book *Utopia* became a black-on-white reality. At that moment the author's idea for the book no longer controlled its content, and a new, different, and collective biography begins—the biography of other people's ideas about what *Utopia* meant. As we shall have occasion to see, some of these ideas bear little visible trace of consanguinity with More's idea for *Utopia*. But our attention to this other and collective biography will be casual and incidental, emerging only when we must pry it off the biography of More's idea for *Utopia*, which it sometimes covers and obscures.

The life span of the idea for *Utopia* is brief. Although there is no precise record of its birth date, it seems to have been born in the mind of Thomas More sometime in the third quarter of 1515; but the event may have taken place a little earlier. The idea was embalmed in print just a little more than a year after its birth. As a biographer I shall naturally have to take into account the environment in which our subject passed its life, and that environment was the mind of Thomas More *between the summer of 1515 and the fall of 1516*. Although we can be sure that that mind was not altogether different from the mind of Thomas More in 1505 or in 1535, we will not commit ourselves to the notion that it was absolutely identical with either of those minds. Indeed, we know for a fact that in one important matter at least it changed sometime in 1518.[1] One further restriction: The mind of

[1] See below, Part Three, section 8.

More is a big, broad, wonderful land. In it the idea for *Utopia* knocked about for above a year, taking its form and shape from its contact with More's general underlying feelings about life and the good life, from his more specific and exact beliefs, and from his momentary reactions to the course of events in which he was at that time involved. We are not, however, concerned with the whole of More's mind at the time but only with that part which impinged on the subject of our biographical sketch—the idea for *Utopia.* The rest of that great intellectual and moral expanse may interest us profoundly but it has no bearing on the subject of this study. Finally a caveat: To establish the lineaments of the idea for *Utopia* we shall perforce, for lack of better sources of information, rely on the book called *Utopia.* But let us not deceive ourselves. The laying out into cold print of what began as a warm living idea always has about it a touch of the mortician's art. Convention requires that the dead letter conform to certain established proprieties, and quite unconsciously an author preparing his idea for interment between covers may impart to it an appearance that it did not wear in life. This, as we shall see, is precisely what the author did with his idea for *Utopia,* and unwary physiognomists examining the corpse have thus read into the living idea lineaments of character which it did not possess. We ourselves shall have to look very closely to separate the thinker's thought from the literary trick of trade.

The printed book we must look at, Sir Thomas More's *Utopia,* was first published at Louvain in 1516 in the Latin in which he wrote it.[2] It was not translated into English dur-

[2] Libellus Vere Aureus nec
MINUS SALUTARIS QUAM FESTI-
uus de optimo reip. statu, deque noua Insula Vtopia
authore clarissimo viro Thoma Moro inclytae
ciutatis Londinensis ciue & vicecomiti cu-
ra M. Petri Aegidi Antwerpiẽsis, & arte

ing the author's lifetime. The first English translation was made by Ralph Robinson and published in 1551.[3] *Utopia* has since found two other translators.[4] Whatever may be the relative merits of the translations, we need not concern ourselves with the later ones. The Robinson rendering alone is readily accessible to present-day readers. Indeed, if we except a handful of scholars, *Utopia* is now known to the English-speaking world only through that rendering. Concerning Robinson's general fidelity to the spirit of More's Latin I cannot speak with much authority. Competent critics have complained that his loose-jointed, somewhat riotous prose destroys the sense of gravity present in the original. This may be so, although in justice to the translator it should be said that his free-and-easy style does not vary a great deal from More's own style in his rather solemn *Dialogue of Comfort*. Perhaps the difference is due less to the spirit of the translator than to the flavor of Tudor English as against humanist Latin. Be that as it may, there are undeniably places where Robinson deviates not merely from the spirit but from the letter and clear meaning of the original; and there are other places where his idiomatic Tudor English, although faithful enough to the original, obscures its meaning for many present-day readers.

For the writer of a study like the one to follow, the situation just outlined presents a technical dilemma. He will have

---

Theodorici Martini Alustensis, Ty
pographi almae Louaniensium
Academiae nunc primum
accuratissime edi
tus .˙.
Cum Gratia et Privilegio

[3] Thomas More, *Utopia*, tr. Ralph Robinson, London, 1551.

[4] Frank and M. P. Sullivan, *Moreana 1478-1945*, Kansas City, 1946, s.v. *Utopia*, indicates only three translations, Robinson's, Gilbert Burnet's in 1684, and G. C. Richard's in 1923. A number of revisions and modernizations of the Robinson and Burnet translations have been published.

to quote frequently from *Utopia.* Quotation from any version but the Robinson translation would inconvenience the reader, since other versions are not easy to come by. On the other hand there are places where an accurate modern rendering of the original is essential to the argument. To meet this situation it has been necessary to adopt a rather unorthodox technical device. All quotations hereafter will follow the Robinson translation with modernized spelling except where a word, phrase, or sentence has had to be retranslated from the Latin in order to give its true meaning or to render it easily intelligible. In those cases the retranslation will appear embedded in the Robinson version, but will be printed in italics. In the footnotes, to justify the retranslation, both the original Latin and the Robinson version will be given.

In the same way, wherever possible Nichols' translation of Erasmus' epistles[5] will be quoted in the text, and the device described above will be used in the one or two instances where a re-rendering has seemed desirable.

One final technical point: A considerable part of the following study depends on a close analysis of *Utopia* itself, so whoever wishes to follow the argument at all will probably want to do so with a copy of *Utopia* at hand to refer to. There are, however, too many editions of *Utopia* available to warrant giving the page references to citations for all of them. References will therefore be given for two of the cheaper editions of the Robinson translation now in print[6] and also for the Lupton edition where Robinson's English and More's

[5] Desiderius Erasmus, *The Epistles of Erasmus from His Earliest Letters to His Fifty-Third Year*, ed. and tr. F. M. Nichols, 3 vols., London, 1901-1918.

[6] Thomas More, *Utopia and Dialogue of Comfort*, Everyman's Library; Thomas More, *Utopia*, ed. J. Churton Collins, Clarendon Press. I have quoted from the Lupton edition which reproduces Robinson's first edition. There are a few minor variants in the Everyman edition which reproduces Robinson's second edition. For the method of notation in footnotes of these and other works frequently noted see Note on Footnote Citations, p. ix.

Latin appear on the same page.[7] Wherever possible in citing Erasmus' correspondence references will be given for both Nichols' English translation and Allen's Latin edition.[8]

[7] Thomas More, *Utopia*, ed. J. H. Lupton, Oxford, 1895. There is another modern Latin edition by Marie Delcourt, Paris, 1942.

[8] Desiderius Erasmus, *Opus Epistolarum Des. Erasmi Roterodami*, ed. P. S. and H. M. Allen, 11 vols., Oxford, 1906-1947.

Part One: The Anatomy of a Printed Book

intention —
is not clear.

Part One: The Anatomy of a Printed Book

1. THE MYSTERY OF *UTOPIA*

More's intentions," in *Utopia*, "must remain mysterious."[1] Thus does the reviewer for the *Times Literary Supplement* end his consideration of two recent works which attempted to explain what Thomas More's intention in the *Utopia* really was.[2] Since the works in question did in fact arrive at rather divergent conclusions as to the nature of that intention, the reviewer's resigned bewilderment is understandable.

A little more difficult to accept is the general implication of the review that the mysteriousness of the author's intent in *Utopia* is somehow a point in his favor, that the obscurity of his meaning enhances the merit of his work. The one point of unanimous agreement about *Utopia* is that it is a work of social comment; and while ambiguity may enhance the value of certain special kinds of poetry, it does not enhance the value of social comment. We should think rather poorly of any present-day social thinker whose intention was inscrutable or mysterious, and unintelligibility is no more a virtue in a criticism of society written four hundred years ago than it is in current social criticism. If it is impossible to know what More means, it is hard to justify the favor that *Utopia* has enjoyed in the past four centuries.

Yet the existence today of the widest divergences of opinion as to More's intent is undeniable, and itself calls for explanation. The number of possible explanations is not great. For some reason More may have purposely concealed or clouded

[1] *Times Literary Supplement*, 3 March 1950, p. 140.

[2] Russell Ames, *Citizen Thomas More and His Utopia*, Princeton, 1949; H. W. Donner, *Introduction to Utopia*, London, 1945.

his intention in *Utopia*. Or he may never have had a very clear notion of his own meaning. Or through literary incompetence he may have failed to express intelligibly a meaning that was clear in his own mind. Or, of course, his intention may be quite clearly expressed in *Utopia*. In the last instance we should have to suppose that something—perhaps the passage of four hundred years and the blinding sandstorms raised by the winds of doctrine—has obscured his meaning to present-day scholars.

The last alternative has a number of points to recommend it. In the first place, no satisfactory reason why More should have concealed his general intent has ever been offered.[3] Second, his gifts both intellectual and literary were on the highest level, and ordinarily he seems to have experienced little trouble either in knowing exactly what he meant or in saying clearly what he knew. Moreover, the divergence of opinion as to his intent is itself of relatively recent vintage—barely a hundred years old. More's contemporaries had no doubt that they knew what he meant in *Utopia*; and—what is a great deal more important—they were in substantial agreement as to what his meaning was.[4] Finally, the methods by which some present-day writers have arrived at their divergent opinions are not above criticism. They have tended

[3] The circumstance that *Utopia* was not printed in England but on the continent has been used to suggest that More feared the consequences of its publication. It is actually of no more significance than the publication of a book by an Indianapolis author of today in New York. Indianapolis now and London then had publishing houses but not major ones. Louvain, Paris, and Basel, where the first three editions of *Utopia* were printed, were, on the other hand, capitals of the publishing trade. And of course More did not doubt that his book would circulate in England. In fact he assisted its circulation there by passing out gift copies. As to attempts to conceal his meaning, no concealed meaning has ever been suggested for any passage of *Utopia* more devastatingly critical of the great and powerful than the explicit statements of a number of passages whose meaning no one has ever disputed or doubted.

[4] See below, Part Two, section 3.

to treat *Utopia* as a grab-bag of ideas. This enables each writer to pull out the ideas that best suit his own taste, to exalt those ideas above the others, and thus to impute to More a hierarchy of conceptions elegantly coincident with the writer's own predilection.

Since *Utopia* is a work of many ideas, it is impossible of course to expound the book unless one has some notion of the hierarchy of conceptions in it. Unfortunately much recent discussion has been marked by a refusal to look for that hierarchy in *Utopia* itself. At worst, as we just noted, the ordering of the ideas in the book has been entirely arbitrary, a sufficient index to the commentator's interests and prepossessions but not to More's. At best the ordering is given a specious solidity by attaching it to one view or another of the total significance of More's life. Now More's life undeniably may throw some light on his intention in *Utopia*. We are in no way rejecting the assistance that light may afford when we say that to determine the meaning of a didactic work the first thing to examine closely is the work itself, the second the circumstances of the writer at the time he wrote it, and only third the overall character of his life. Books are often simple and direct, while the lives of men run to complexity and ambivalence. To make the interpretation of a book depend on a full understanding of the life of its author is often to make what is easy to determine depend on what is hard or impossible to achieve.[5] A careful reading of *Utopia* does seem to

[5] Although I agree with Oncken (Thomas More, *Utopia*, tr. by G. Ritter, intro. by H. Oncken, Berlin, 1922) as to the desirability of a careful examination of the text of *Utopia* in view of the peculiar history of its composition, I do not agree with his and his followers' particular analysis, which, for one thing, seems too far at variance with the external evidence on the composition of the work (see below, Part One, section 4). The significance read into Oncken's analysis by himself and his followers is too fantastic to warrant treatment here, particularly since it has been completely discredited recently by Donner's careful discussion (Donner, pp. 60-66, 98-100). My complete disagreement with Oncken's interpreta-

me to reveal clearly the hierarchy of its author's ideas at the time he composed the book. Some of these ideas are casual and peripheral, others crucial to the work, giving it point and coherence. It also seems to me that the circumstances of the author when he wrote *Utopia* confirm the view of his intent derived from reading the book, and that the events of More's life do not reveal any discrepancy between the intent ascribed to *Utopia* and the career of its author.

The conception of More's meaning in *Utopia* shortly to be set forth is unimpeachably orthodox; it coincides precisely with the opinion of those contemporaries of More who were most likely to judge his meaning aright.[6] We cannot, however, just quote his contemporaries and let it go at that. For the men first to write about *Utopia* did not feel it necessary to state More's line of argument in full, believing perhaps that he had already done that better than they could. Nor did they look beneath the surface of his thought for the nexus of ideas and feelings that gave his social comment its unique coherence; they were concerned with the outcome rather than the nature of More's way of thinking. Besides they felt no need to prove that their conception of More's intent was correct, since it had never been challenged. The success of a whole congeries of heresies about *Utopia* in the past hundred years, however, has thrown the burden of proof on the advocate of a neo-orthodoxy.

Although the interpretation of *Utopia* which follows has no pretensions to substantial novelty, but rather disavows it, my approach to the problem may seem singular and ec-

---

tion of More's intent in the *Utopia* and my considerable disagreement with his analysis of its composition doubles my chagrin at being anticipated by him on one point. My illusion that I was the first to notice a break in Book I of *Utopia* (see below, Part One, section 3) was shattered by a subsequent reading of Oncken's introduction to the Ritter German translation, pp. 11*-12*.

[6] See below, Part Two, section 3.

centric. The structure of a work so long famous should hold no unsolved mysteries after four hundred years, and it may seem presumptuous to suggest that much about the meaning of *Utopia* can be learned at this late date from anything so pedestrian as a reconstruction of the history of its composition. Yet a careful analysis of the literary structure of *Utopia*, although it throws no new light on the meaning of the work, may dispel some of the dimness in which the passage of four hundred years has enveloped a very old light. The account of such an analysis will necessarily be a little dull, so I shall have to request the forbearance of the reader without even being able to promise him for his patience any large reward in the shape of a brand new insight.

2. SEARCH FOR A NARRATOR

It is well established that More worked out a large part of *Utopia* while in the Netherlands in 1515 as a member of a mission that Henry VIII sent there to negotiate with the representatives of Prince Charles, later Charles V.[1] It is equally certain that he finished the published version of the work in England by September 1516, when he sent the finished manuscript to his intimate friend, the great Dutch humanist Erasmus, who saw it through the press.[2] It is Erasmus himself who tells us that it was Book II of the published version of *Utopia* that was written first in the Netherlands, and that More added Book I after his return to England.[3] Granted the general reliability of all this, can we take Erasmus' statement, written a number of years after the

[1] This is a legitimate inference from More's dedicatory letter to Giles and the first few pages of *Utopia* itself; L 1-12, 21-25, E 7-14, C 250-254, 1-2 (see Note on Footnote Citations, p. ix). Any earlier date for any part of the work is made improbable by the mention in Book II of the *Glossariam Graecum* of Hesychius, first published in Venice in 1514 (L 216, note 1).

[2] N 2:381; A 2:461, line 1 (see Note on Footnote Citations, p. ix).

[3] N 3:398; A 4:999, lines 259-260

event in an epistolary biography of More, to be literally accurate in detail? Was it just Book II and all of Book II that More wrote in the Netherlands, just Book I and all of Book I that he wrote in England? An examination of *Utopia* itself may provide an answer to this question; so let us first inspect Book II, according to Erasmus the earlier-written part.

Without prefatory remark Book II begins with a physical description of the Island of Utopia.[4] In succeeding chapters the details of the way of life of the Utopians are expounded.[5] Then comes a sort of peroration or summing up,[6] and finally a concluding section.[7] In this last brief section for the first time in Book II More mentions the name of the narrator of the account of Utopia: it is Raphael; his last name is not given.[8] Up to this very last bit of Book II, no narrator, no Raphael has been mentioned. Who is this Raphael, and where does he come from? We know of course that he is Raphael Hythloday, who is introduced very fully as the narrator in Book I.[9] But then what is he doing in Book II, which was presumably written before Book I? There are two possible explanations of the sudden appearance of Hythloday as narrator at the very end of Book II. Neither, however, is compatible with that sharp dividing line between the two Books in chronology of composition, which a literal interpretation of Erasmus' statement suggests.

The first explanation would suppose that all of Book I and the last section of Book II were written after More returned to London. This would imply that Raphael Hythloday, the narrator in the finished version, had not been invented when the body of Book II was worked out in the Netherlands, but was created later when More wrote Book I. To this hypothesis

[4] L 115-119, E 48-49, C 48-50 [5] L 119-298, E 49-110, C 50-138
[6] L 298-307, E 110-114, C 138-143 [7] L 307-309, E 114-115, C 143-144
[8] "Thus when Raphael had made an end of his tale . . ." L 307, E 114, C 143
[9] L 25-29, E 14-16, C 2-5

there are serious objections. In the first place the account of Utopia in Book II is not an impersonal description such as one might find in a present-day social and economic geography book. It is a traveler's tale, a personal narration by a narrator with strong opinions, an "I" who pops up occasionally in the course of the account;[10] and this narrator has been to Utopia. There is also an audience in Book II, a "you" ostensibly listening to the narrative;[11] and this audience has *not* been to Utopia. Now it is most improbable that More would have equipped his description of Utopia with both a narrator and an audience from the outset and yet never have bothered to identify either one or the other. But on the first hypothesis—that all of Book I was written in England—this is what we should have to suppose.

The improbability of the first hypothesis is increased when we note that besides his personal opinions Book II contains a few bits of autobiographical information about the narrator. He lived for *five years* in Amaurote,[12] the head town of the Utopian federation. He connects his stay in Utopia with the last of *four* voyages he has made.[13] He displays his own preferences by recommending *Greek* but not Latin literature to the attention of the Utopians.[14] He says that in Utopia he and his companions made up a party of four, although originally they were *six*.[15] Now very early in Book I we are introduced to the wandering philosopher, Raphael Hythloday, and in the course of Book I we are informed among other things that Hythloday lived in Utopia for *five years*,[16] that

[10] "I will describe," *Depingam*, L 126, E 51, C 53; "I . . . saw," *viderim*, L 131, E 53, C 55; "as I said," *ut dixi*, L 139, E 55, C 59; "I say," *inquam*, L 140, E 55, C 59.

[11] "lest you be deceived," *ne quid erretis*, L 145, E 57, C 61; "Now you see," *Jam videtis*, L 169, E 65, C 74.

[12] L 126, E 51, C 53

[13] L 215, E 81, C 96

[14] L 213, E 81, C 95

[15] L 269, E 101, C 124

[16] L 110, E 45, C 46

he had accompanied Amerigo Vespucci on all *four* of the latter's voyages,[17] that he prefers *Greek* authors to Latin,[18] that on his last journey with Vespucci he had stayed behind with the garrison there, and that later he left the garrison and in a party of *six* traveled widely by land and sea into unknown countries.[19] The obvious inference to be drawn from these parallels and coincidences provides us with an alternative and more satisfactory hypothesis to explain the sudden appearance of Raphael Hythloday at the end of Book II. He had in fact been there throughout the Book. Hythloday was part of the original conception of the *Utopia* and was not added later. But if this is true, then along with Book II some part of Book I must have been written before More came back to England from the Netherlands.

3. THE CURIOUS PARAGRAPH

But what part? Can we determine more precisely what portions of Book I were composed along with Book II? Let us start at the beginning of Book I. A few of the preliminary details were probably set down after More's return to England—perhaps the eulogy of Tunstall, certainly the detail of his appointment to be Master of the Rolls.[1] From the introduction of the author's journey to Antwerp,[2] however, we reach the part—introducing both Hythloday and the linked references—that we have already connected with Book II as written in the Netherlands, and the only question is how far into Book I this part penetrates. We see no sign of a break until we come to a curious paragraph which I will have to quote almost in full:

"What he [Hythloday] told us that he saw in every country

[17] L 27, E 15, C 4 [18] L 27, E 15, C 3 [19] L 28, E 15, C 4

[1] L 22, E 13, C 1. The appointment was actually made after the mission returned from the Netherlands.

[2] L 23-24, E 14, C 2

where he came, it were very long to declare—*nor is that the design of this work.*[3] But peradventure in another place I will speak of it, chiefly such things as shall be profitable to be known, as in special be those decrees and ordinances, that he marked to be well and wisely provided and enacted among such peoples as do live together in a civil policy and good order. For of such things did we busily inquire. . . . As he marked many fond and foolish laws in those new found lands, so he rehearsed many acts and constitutions whereby these our cities, nations, countries and kingdoms may take example to amend their faults, enormities, and errors. Whereof in another place, as I said, I will treat. Now at this time I am determined to rehearse only what he told us of the manners, customs, laws, and ordinances of the Utopians."[4]

Several of the assertions here requires special emphasis: (1) Hythloday told of other lands besides Utopia.[5] (2) He spoke especially of things "profitable to be known" concerning "decrees and ordinances" of peoples living together "in civil policy and good order."[6] (3) The profit of rehearsing such information would lie in the example "our cities, nations, countries, and kingdoms" could take from it "to amend their faults, enormities, and errors."[7] *But* (4) this is not what More is going to tell about now. He assures us of this thrice over. Such is not "the design of this work."[8] Again, "Peradventure in another place I will speak of it."[9] Again, "In another place I will treat of these matters."[10] He says he is postponing these other matters because (5) "Now at this time I am determined to rehearse only what he told us of the manners, customs, laws and ordinances of the Utopians."[11]

Now I have said that this paragraph is curious. Yet it is not

[3] "Neither is it my purpose at this time to make rehearsal thereof," *neque huius est operis institutum,* L 32, E 17, C 6

[4] L 32-34, E 17, C 6-7 [5] L 32, E 17, C 6 [6] L 33, E 17, C 6

[7] L 34, E 17, C 7 [8] L 32, E 17, C 6 [9] L 33, E 17, C 6

[10] L 34, E 17, C 7 [11] L 34, E 17, C 7

intrinsically curious. It looks like a fairly straightforward prospectus of what is immediately to follow—no tales about the various countries Hythloday talked about, no attempt to draw lessons from them for the correction of European realms, simply an account of the Utopian commonwealth. The odd point is entirely extrinsic: for what we are told will follow does *not* immediately follow, and what we are told will not follow *does* immediately follow. For the rest of Book I we hear very little of the manners, customs, laws, and ordinances of the Utopians, and for five-sixths of that Book we hear nothing whatever about their institutions.[12] Instead we hear, among other matters, of "the decrees and ordinances" of three other peoples among whom Hythloday had traveled, three peoples who "live together in a civil policy and good order"—the Polylerites,[13] the Achorians,[14] and the Macarians.[15] And "their decrees and ordinances" are quite specifically held up as an example "whereby our kingdoms may . . . amend their faults, enormities, and errors." In a summing up at the end of this discussion Hythloday in effect sums up the peculiar inconsistency too:

"This communication of mine, though peradventure it may seem unpleasant to [kings and their councilors] yet can I not see why it should seem strange, or foolishly newfangled. If so be that I should speak those things that Plato feigneth in his weal public, or that the Utopians do in theirs, these things though they were (as they be indeed) better, yet they might

[12] There are 30 pages of the first book of *Utopia* after the "curious paragraph" in the Everyman edition (E 17-47); in the Lupton edition, 80 pages (L 34-114); in the Clarendon, 40 pages (C 7-47). The first observation on Utopian institutions occurs 25 pages after the "curious paragraph" in the Everyman (E 42), 67 pages after in the Lupton edition (L 101), 34 pages after in the Clarendon (C 41). In the meantime Utopia is twice mentioned, but only for purposes of geographical identification. L 85, 95; E 36, 40; C 33, 38

[13] L 64-71, E 28-31, C 22-26

[14] L 85-87, E 36-37, C 33-34

[15] L 95-97, E 40, C 38-39

seem spoken out of place. Forasmuch as here amongst us every man has his possessions several to himself, and there all things be common. But what was in my communication contained that might not, and ought not in any place be spoken? Saving that to them which have thoroughly decreed and determined with themselves to run headlong the contrary way it cannot be acceptable and pleasant, because it calleth them back, and showeth them the jeopardies."[16]

Here almost at the close of Book I the Utopians are mentioned for the first time since the end of the curious paragraph.

4. RECONSTRUCTION OF *UTOPIA*

The inconsistency between the prospectus in the curious paragraph and the subject matter that follows in the printed version of *Utopia* becomes intelligible if we make a few assumptions about the development of the book's composition. In what he wrote in the Netherlands More had launched Hythloday on his description of Utopia just after our curious paragraph.[1] After all, as a prospectus of what appears in Book II that paragraph is quite accurate, for Book II "rehearses only what" Hythloday told "of the manners, customs, laws, and ordinances of the Utopians." When More came back to London he wrote his later addition and then had to find a place for it. So he pried open a seam at the place where Hythloday's discourse originally had begun and inserted the addition there. He hooked the addition onto the previously written introduction—weakly enough it seems to me—by the sentence, "But first I will repeat our former communication by the occasion and . . . drift whereof" Hythloday came to mention Utopia.[2] On this hypothesis Book I from the end of

[16] L 100-101, E 42, C 41

[1] L 32-34, E 17, C 6-7

[2] L 34, E 17, C 7

the curious paragraph on would be what More later added to *Utopia*.

Up to a point within a very few pages of the end of Book I this reconstruction offers no difficulties, since up to that point we listen to a coherent and continuous argument among Hythloday, Giles, and More.[3] The argument, however, finally reaches a conclusion or at least an impasse, and abruptly the whole line of discourse changes. Up to this point, as we have seen, Hythloday has been holding forth on a number of things that the rulers of European lands should and *could* do to bring their commonwealths into a better order after the example of the Polylerites, the Macarians, and the Achorians. He has had little to say about Utopia, and only once very casually has he mentioned community of property, the most marked institutional peculiarity of the Utopians.[4] Now he suddenly takes off at an angle from the course he had set in his previous remarks, and says, "Howbeit doubtless . . . where possessions be private . . . it is hard and almost impossible that there the weal public may justly be governed and prosperously flourish."[5] From this sudden sentence to the end of Book I our attempt to reconstruct the composition of *Utopia* runs into a bit of heavy sledding. Was this concluding section written in England or was it written earlier in the Netherlands? We can only be quite sure that it *is* a section, that from the breakpoint at which Hythloday veers onto the problem of property to the end of Book I we are dealing with a homogeneous piece of writing without an internal break. Now this section of *Utopia* contains one of those paired references—in this case to Hythloday's five years' residence in Utopia[6]—by means of which we have connected the brief introductory section of Book I to the long discourse in Book II as having been written in the Netherlands. The presence of

[3] L 34-104, E 17-43, C 7-43
[4] L 101, E 42, C 41
[5] L 104-105, E 43, C 43
[6] L 110, 126; E 45, 51; C 46, 53

such a paired reference in the concluding section of Book I seems at first sight to suggest that it too was written in the Netherlands.

There are, however, objections to this suggestion. In general, if Hythloday's attack on property is put just after the curious paragraph it makes no sense; the two do not hook up. Yet they should if they were written together in the Netherlands and the dialogue that separates them was inserted later as an afterthought. Specifically there is one bit of action that becomes unintelligible if More wrote the conclusion to Book I in the Netherlands before working out the dialogue. In the introduction More brought Giles and Hythloday back to his house, "and there in my garden *on a grassy bank*[7] we sat down talking together."[8] Now at the very end of the concluding section of Book I in answer to More's request Hythloday says he will gladly tell all about the Utopian commonwealth, but "the matter requireth leisure."[9] So on More's suggestion that the company eat before Hythloday begins, "we went in and dined. When dinner was done, we came into the same place again, and sat us down upon the same *seat*,[10] commanding our servants that no man should trouble us. Then I and Master Peter Giles desired Master Raphael to perform his promise." And so after musing a while Hythloday began his description of the Utopian commonwealth.[11] Now if it was necessary to come back after dinner to hear Raphael tell about Utopia, what had the three men been talking about all morning? In the printed version of *Utopia* the morning is consumed by the dialogue in Book I, but that dialogue was not written until More got back to London. Without it, however, the morning becomes a literary and artistic blank, and the interruption for dinner makes no sense.

[7] "upon a bench covered with green turves," *in scamno cespitibus herbeis constrato*, L 29, E 16, C 4-5

[8] L 29, E 16, C 5

[9] L 114, E 46, C 47

[10] "bench"; *sedile*

[11] L 114, E 46-47, C 47

Our difficulty here vanishes if we assume that no interruption for dinner was contemplated by More when he was writing in the Netherlands because he had not at that time considered introducing the dialogue in Book I. As he had first worked out his *Utopia* the discourse in Book II followed hard upon our curious paragraph in Book I, and this in fact is the most coherent arrangement of the parts. On this hypothesis can we explain the paired reference to Hythloday's stay in Utopia, the pause for dinner, and the abruptness with which the concluding section of Book I begins? I think we can without too much difficulty. We will suppose that sometime after his return to London, and for reasons which we will examine later, More wrote the dialogue in Book I up to the breakpoint. Then he was faced with the problem of hooking this new piece both fore and aft into what he had already written in the Netherlands. We have already seen how he made the fore end fast to the introduction, casually and carelessly enough, yet well enough too, so that to the best of my knowledge the junction point escaped notice for four hundred years. At the aft end he faced two problems. In the first place he had to get Hythloday back from the subject of the dialogue and on to his description of Utopia. In the second place he noticed that with the dialogue he had already pretty well killed the time available for the morning's talk, time originally set aside for the description of Utopia. More decided that the best way to get Hythloday back on the track was to have him make some observation about the Utopian commonwealth that would presumably arouse the curiosity of his auditors. So at the breakpoint he abruptly launches him into a eulogy of the community of all things as practiced in Utopia.[12] This serves the purpose, but it would make the session on the grassy bank inordinately long if Hythloday discoursed of the

[12] L 104, E 43, C 43

Utopian commonwealth right away. Hence the pause for refreshment.

As to the paired reference to Hythloday's five-year stay in Utopia,[13] either of two explanations of its presence are equally possible. In either case it serves to link the part of *Utopia* written in England with that written in the Netherlands—corroborative detail to lend artistic versimilitude to the narrative. Perhaps before working out his end link More glanced through the already complete discourse, noted that he had there assigned five years to Hythloday's stay in Utopia, and repeated the statement when he wrote the end link—the concluding section of Book I. Equally well he may have assigned the length of Hythloday's sojourn among the Utopians when he wrote the end link, and then inserted the equivalent statement into the draft of the discourse.

It is then to turn us away from the subject of the dialogue of Book I and bring us back to the edge of Utopia, from which we had drifted off at the end of the curious paragraph, that More suddenly launches Hythloday into his attack on private property. It needs only for More to put into his own mouth the conventional argument against community of property and goods as a danger to prosperity and public order[14] to allow Hythloday to come around to the point from which he was diverted many pages earlier: "If you had been with me in Utopia and had presently seen their fashions and laws . . . then doubtless you would grant that you never saw people well ordered, but only there."[15] Thence the transition to the description of Utopian institutions of Book II is smooth and easy. Tentatively, then, we suggest that the part of *Utopia* which More composed in London after finishing Book II in the Netherlands begins at the close of our curious paragraph and runs to the end of Book I.[16] This hypothesis at least has

[13] L 110, 126; E 45, 51; C 46, 53
[14] L 109-110, E 45, C 45
[15] L 110-111, E 45, C 45-46
[16] L 34-114, E 17-47, C 7-47

the merit of imputing the maximum possible accuracy to Erasmus' account of the composition of *Utopia.*

It leaves us, however, with one disjected member to dispose of—the concluding brief section of Book II that follows the completion of Hythloday's communication.[17] Now this section contains a back reference. More says that he refrained from challenging any of the ideas Hythloday had expressed, especially because he remembered that Hythloday had "reprehended this fault in others, which be afraid lest they should seem not to be wise enough, unless they could find some fault in other men's inventions."[18]

Where had Hythloday said this? At a point somewhat *after* the curious paragraph in Book I, speaking of royal councils, he says "There the hearers *act*[19] as though the whole estimation of their wisdom were in jeopardy to be overthrown . . . unless they could in other men's inventions pick out matters to reprehend and find fault at."[20] But this last quotation is from the later section of *Utopia,* written after More's return from the Netherlands. If our hypothesis is correct, then the concluding section of Book II of *Utopia* was also probably written at that time.

In summary, then, we propose the following scheme of composition for *Utopia*: A few prefatory lines,[21] Book I from the end of the curious paragraph on,[22] and the concluding section of Book II[23]—written in London some time after More's return from his mission to the Netherlands; the rest[24] written earlier, probably while More was waiting in the Netherlands for Charles' councilors to make the decisions on which his mission depended. This analysis is in some measure

[17] L 307-309, E 114-115, C 143-144
[18] L 308, E 114, C 143
[19] "fare"; *agunt*
[20] L 39, E 19, C 10
[21] L 21 to about ". . . thence to Antwerp," L 24; E 13-14, C 1-2
[22] L 34-114; E 17-47, C 7-47
[23] L 307-309, E 114-115, C 143-144
[24] L 24-34, 115-307; E 14-17, 48-114; C 2-7, 48-143

confirmed both by the over-all structure and by the form of *Utopia.* Structurally the direct transition from the curious paragraph to Book II is simple and natural, involving none of the strained contrivance that we have noted in the organization of the final published work. As to form, one writer observes, "One fact has been overlooked by nearly all commentators upon the *Utopia*; and that is that it was written in the form of a dialogue,"[25] after the model of Plato's *Republic.* To me it seems that this fact is not a fact at all. Book II up to the concluding section, and that means two-thirds of the whole work,[26] is anything but a dialogue; it is an uninterrupted discourse by Hythloday on the Utopian commonwealth. And in what we may now call the original introduction[27] there is no evidence whatever that More initially intended to use the dialogue form. All the dialogue of a Platonic or dialectic sort, then, is in the part of *Utopia* written after More returned to London. He seems to have hit upon dialogue as the natural and appropriate form *for that particular section.* The forms then of what we consider the earlier- and the later-written sections of *Utopia* are internally consistent when taken separately. Combined they are a hodgepodge of discourse and dialogue.

Now for convenience we name the parts in the order in which they occur in the final version of *Utopia,* and assign to each the place where it was composed: Book I—Preface (England), Introduction (Netherlands), Dialogue including the end link (England); Book II—Discourse (Netherlands), Conclusion (England).

Does our analysis, if correct, throw any light on More's intent in *Utopia?* Critics have tended to see in the published

[25] W. E. Campbell, *More's Utopia and His Social Teaching,* London, 1930, p. 25.

[26] In Lupton, 193 pages against 95 for the rest of the work, in Everyman, 66 against 35, in Clarendon, 96 against 47.

[27] L 24-34, E 14-17, C 2-7

book a unified literary design, and to treat it as if it were the consistent working out of a preconceived plan; but our breakdown of its construction suggests another possibility. The part of *Utopia* that More composed first is itself a consistent, coherent, and practically complete literary work. This implies —what I believe to be true—that in More's original intent the first-written part of *Utopia*, probably completed in Antwerp, *was* a finished work, that only after he returned to London did he feel impelled to add anything to it, that the published version of *Utopia* falls into two parts which represent two different and separate sets of intention on the part of the author, the first embodied in the finished book he carried back from the Netherlands, the second in the additions he later made in England.

This hypothesis does not have to rest altogether on internal evidence. Only two significant pieces of contemporary external evidence on the composition of *Utopia* survive. Luckily both bear on the point we are seeking to make. When More sent the final version of *Utopia* to Erasmus to get it published, he enclosed a letter to Peter Giles of Antwerp, who figures so prominently in the book itself as to leave no reasonable doubt that he was—as it were—in at the birth. It begins:

"I am almost ashamed, right well-beloved Peter Giles, to send unto you this book of the Utopian commonwealth, well-nigh after a year's space which I am sure you looked for within a month and a half. And no marvel. For you knew well enough that I was already disburdened of all the labor and study belonging to the invention in this work, and that I had no need at all to trouble my brains about the disposition or conveyance of the matter: and therefore had herein nothing else to do but only to rehearse those things which you and I together heard Master Raphael tell and declare."[28]

There is a touch of obliqueness about this opening because

[28] L 1-2, E 7, C 250

More is using it along with the rest of the letter to add to the sense of reality with which he surrounds his imaginary narrator, Hythloday. Despite the obliqueness however it is clear that Giles had reason to expect to see *Utopia* within six weeks of More's departure either from Antwerp or from the Netherlands. But six weeks seems little enough time to allow a busy man for polishing and correcting a manuscript and for getting a clean copy of it made. Under the circumstances Giles could hardly have expected to see *Utopia* so soon again unless he had already seen it practically complete. That he did in fact believe the work to be almost complete before his friend More went back to England is precisely what More's letter indicates. But that this well-nigh finished book could not have been the published version is clear from what Erasmus has to say about the composition of *Utopia.* Describing to Hutten how More went about putting the published version together, he says, "*he had written the second book at his leisure, and afterward because of a particular situation he added the first part on the spur of the moment.*"[29] The *occasio* for the later-written part of the *Utopia* was certainly not literary or esthetic since the dialogue disturbs the esthetic unity of the book; the impulsion, whatever its source, was external, extrinsic to the work itself. What that *occasio* was we shall later have to inquire.[30] For the present Erasmus' statement taken with the letter to Giles and the structure of the published edition provides us with sufficient evidence that the *Utopia* that was complete in More's mind and intention when he left the Netherlands was not the whole published work but only the discourse that comprises the bulk of Book II plus the introduction in Book I that we have already isolated.

[29] *Secundum librum prius scripserat per ocium, mox per occasionem primum adiecet ex tempore,* Erasmus to Hutten, "He had written the second book at his leisure, and afterwards when he found it was required added the first offhand," N 3:398, A 4:999, lines 259-260

[30] See below, Part Three, section I.

Well, if this is all true, what of it? Suppose that the parts of *Utopia* that we describe as first-written stood in More's mind as a complete work when he had finished them—does this tell us anything of his broader meaning, of his general intent in writing *Utopia?* I think perhaps it does. To investigate the relation between the structure of *Utopia* and the meaning and intent of its author is in large part the purpose of this little book.

Part Two: The Discourse of Utopia

Part Two: The Discourse of Utopia

1. PROPERTY IN THE DISCOURSE

THE conclusions various scholars have come to about More's attitude toward the institution of property coincide to a remarkable degree with their own predilections on that point, or with their notions of what More should have thought if he was the kind of man they suppose him to be. Thus for Karl Kautsky *Utopia* is a socialist vision—and to a considerable extent a Marxian socialist vision—far in advance of its time.[1] In the same way, but in a different sense, several recent Catholic scholars have written of More's social views as if he formed them with the encyclicals *Rerum Novarum* and *Quinquagesimo Anno* in mind.[2] And the most recent Marxist interpretation, subtler than Kautsky's, relegates More's views on private property to a secondary place in his social philosophy on the grounds that More was a "middle class man," and that the important part of his thought is that which conforms to the writer's notion of what an "enlightened" sixteenth century bourgeois should think.[3] Many scholars indeed have been so anxious to square More's views on property with their own that they have paid only casual attention either to what More himself said about property in *Utopia* or to how he said it. Yet he had a great deal to say about property there, and it seems to me that an examination of the way he said it can settle as determinatively as such things can be settled what his beliefs on the subject were at the time he wrote *Utopia*. It is at this point that the analysis of *Utopia* which we have just attempted may prove

[1] Karl Kautsky, *Thomas More and His Utopia*, with a Historical Introduction, tr. H. J. Stenning, N.Y., 1927, passim

[2] Campbell, passim

[3] Ames, passim

helpful. It enables us to isolate the views that More expressed in the Netherlands in the work of his first intention from his opinions as he formulated them almost a year later in the additions he made in England. The usefulness of the analysis will be apparent if we apply it to a hypothesis about More's attitude on the institution of property which at present is enjoying a considerable vogue.

In *Utopia* More put the only criticisms of community of property and the only defenses of private property into his own mouth. Because of this coincidence it is argued that these criticisms rather than Hythloday's praise represent the author's own true opinion.[4] If the analysis of the structure of *Utopia* just set forth is correct, this contention falls flat not once but twice. For there is no defense of private property at all in the *Utopia* of More's first intention, that is, in the Introduction and Discourse written in the Netherlands. The climax and conclusion of that work is Hythloday's magnificent peroration against private property with its theme unmistakably stated at the outset:

[4] Campbell, pp. 25-29. Campbell repeats this argument almost verbatim in "The *Utopia* of Sir Thomas More," *The King's Good Servant*, Westminster, Md., 1948, pp. 26-39. The fullest elaboration of this argument will be found in Donner, pp. 66-75.

I had almost completed an appendix subjecting to close examination evidence presented by Donner in support of the thesis that in *Utopia* More dissociated himself from the views on private property expressed by Hythloday when my colleague Prof. George Parks brought to my attention an excellent article dealing with that evidence by Edward L. Surtz, S.J., "Thomas More and Communism," *PMLA*, 64, 1949, pp. 549-564. The article makes such an appendix redundant. Father Surtz demonstrates that the passages cited by Donner are quite irrelevant to the case they are intended to support, since they do not deal with the community of property as practiced in Utopia at all (pp. 562-564). He also presents independent evidence as to More's views on communism from More's writings composed within a very few years of the composition of *Utopia* (pp. 553, 559-562). One passage he cites confirms the view that More attached great importance to the ideal of the community of property (p. 553), and that *Utopia* is unintelligible unless we recognize that ideal as central to More's conception of "the best state of a commonwealth."

"Now I have declared and described unto you, as truly as I could, the form and order of that commonwealth, which verily in my judgment is not only the best, but also that which alone of good right may claim and take upon it the name of a commonwealth or public weal. For in other places they speak still of the commonwealth. But every man procureth his own private wealth. Here where nothing is private, the common affairs be earnestly looked upon."[5]

As he develops his theme he castigates every European realm: "Therefore when I consider and weigh in my mind all these commonwealths which nowadays anywhere do flourish, so God help me, I can perceive nothing but a certain conspiracy of rich men procuring their own commodities under the name and title of the common wealth."[6]

Finally the Utopian community of property and goods which plucks up by the roots the great occasion for wickedness and mischief is "gladly wished" to all nations.[7] On that note of praise for community of property and goods the original *Utopia—Utopia* as More first intended it—ends.

2. MORE'S "DEFENSE" OF PRIVATE PROPERTY

Still it may be argued that when More got back to England he had a sober second thought. He realized that from *Utopia* as it stood someone might draw the inference which we in fact just drew. To prevent just such a calamity, when he added the new sections to the book he carefully put not one but two defenses of private property into his own mouth.

Perhaps the best way to evaluate this contention is to set down next to each other those two defenses of private property. Here they are:

"*Their common life and community of living without any traffic in money, this alone, which is the ultimate foundation*

[5] L 299, E 110-111, C 138 [6] L 303, E 112, C 140 [7] L 306, E 114, C 142

of all their institutions, overthrows all excellence, magnificence, splendor, and majesty—the true proprieties and distinctions of a commonwealth according to the common opinion."[1]

"Men shall never live there wealthily, where all things be common. For how can there be abundance of goods, or of anything, where every man withdraweth his hand from labor. Whom the regard of his own gain driveth not to work and the hope that he hath of other men's travails maketh him slothful. Then when they be pricked with poverty, and yet no man can by any law or right defend that for his own, which he hath gotten with the labor of his own hands, shall not there of necessity be continual sedition and bloodshed? Specially the authority and reverence of magistrates being taken away, which what place it may have with such men among whom *there are no gradations of rank,*[2] I cannot devise."[3]

Now there is an enormous difference between these two critiques of community of property and goods. The second argument is serious and consequential. It proposes difficulties that any communal scheme must take account of. The first argument, on the other hand, is simply vapid and frivolous. Frivolous not only from a present-day point of view, but from More's own point of view and that of every contemporary of his who thought seriously about politics. Not one of those contemporaries would have maintained for a moment that what mattered in a commonwealth were splendor, magnifi-

[1] "in that which is the principal foundation of all their ordinances, that is to say, in the community of their life and living, without any occupying of money; by the which thing only all nobility, magnificence, worship, honor, and majesty, the true ornaments and honors, as the common opinion is, of a common wealth, utterly be overthrown and destroyed," *quod maximum totius institutionis fundamentum est, uita scilicet uictuque communi, sine ullo pecuniae commercio, qua una re funditus euertitur omnis nobilitas, magnificentia, splendor, maiestas, uera (ut publica est opinio) decora atque ornamenta Reipublicae,* L 308, E 114, C 143

[2] "is no difference"; *nullum discrimen est*

[3] L 109-110, E 45, C 45

cence, and majesty.[4] What mattered to them were order, harmony, justice, peace, and prosperity. In *Utopia* and elsewhere, with a vehemence that does not leave his conviction in doubt, More has set down his own estimate of the role that splendor, magnificence, and majesty play in this world. The rich and royal psalmist, King David, he tells us in the *Dialogue of Comfort*, most highly distinguishes himself not when he displays a glorious pomp, but when "he taketh his wealth for no wealth, nor his riches for no riches, nor in his heart setteth by neither nother, but secretly liveth in a contrite heart and a life penitential."[5]

More's contempt for earthly magnificence and splendor appears not only in his earnest direct denunciations of it in *Utopia*,[6] and in his elimination of all pomp from his ideal commonwealth except in connection with religious worship,[7] but also in his humorous asides, and particularly in his autobiographical aside about the mission of the ambassadors of Anemolia—Land of the Windy Ones—to Utopia. Those splendid and magnificent emissaries, bearers of the majesty of the Anemolians, came to Utopia "determined in the gorgeousness of their apparel to represent very gods."[8] They wore luxurious cloth of gold "with great chains of gold, with gold hanging at their ears, with gold rings upon their fingers, with broaches and *pendants*[9] of gold upon their caps, which glistened full of pearls and precious stones," in order "with the bright shining and glistening of their gay clothing to dazzle the eyes of the silly poor Utopians."[10] Thus splendidly and magnificently got up they paraded through the capital town of Amaurote; but the Utopians had their own ideas

[4] e.g., Claude Seyssel, *Grant Monarchie de France*, Paris, 1519, passim

[5] E 176

[6] L 45-47, 56-57, 107, 145-152, 300-303; E 21-22, 25, 44, 57-60, 111-112; C 13, 18, 44, 61-65, 139-140

[7] *Utopia*, Book II, passim

[8] L 178, E 69, C 78-79

[9] "aglettes"; *appensis*

[10] L 178-179, E 69, C 79

about such pompous shows. In Utopia gold chains were for slaves, and precious stones were baubles for children.[11] So the magnificent and splendid Anemolian ambassadors had the joy of hearing young Utopians say to their mothers in wonder: "Look mother how great a lubber doth yet wear pearls and *gems*,[12] as though he were a little child still. But the mother, yea and that also in good earnest: peace, son, sayeth she: I think he be some of the ambassadors' fools."[13]

It is a tale that in 1515 More can tell wryly with a mixture of amusement and ruefulness, since a few months before as ambassador of His splendid and magnificent Majesty, the King of England, he himself had to parade through Bruges bedecked and bedizened as the Anemolian emissaries were. And although it is unlikely that any Flemish child on that occasion called poor More a lubber, there was little need to; no doubt he felt a great enough lubber nevertheless.[14]

Indeed More's revulsion against pomp and display is embedded in levels of his being deeper than his discriminating intellect and rational consciousness. It stems from reasons of his heart and temperament that reason does not know. Not only the most eloquent passages of *Utopia* but his whole life and character are a living and total repudiation on his part of the conspicuous consumption and the false and invidious discriminations implied for him in the terms, "magnificence, splendor, majesty." When he carefully selects that particular group of words to support his "defense" of private property, we may justly suspect the sincerity of his ardor for the cause. Under the circumstances it is really not a defense at all; it is simply treason within the citadel.

[11] L 175-177, E 68, C 77-78
[12] "precious stones"; *gemmis*
[13] L 180, E 69-70, C 80
[14] I am indebted to Prof. Garrett Mattingly of Columbia University for pointing out to me the personal poignancy this passage must have had for More, still Ambassador to the Netherlands when he wrote it in 1515.

Now if anyone honestly wanted to uphold private property, surely he would rest his case with a mature, not with a palpably silly and insincere, argument. More does the opposite. Against Hythloday's magnificent invective hurled at private property at the end of Book II, he sets not the serious but the silly defense of it. This juxtaposition at the very end of the published version of *Utopia* leaves the reader with a feeling of disgust at the evils of private property. This is precisely the effect that anyone in his good senses would expect from such an ending, and More was certainly in his good senses when he wrote it.

Of course More could not put the serious argument against community of property at the end of Book II, because he had already used it near the end of Book I.[15] But why? He wrote both arguments at approximately the same time; why did he make the weak argument the final one? If he was really defending an important position, why did he shoot off all his heavy artillery ammunition before the enemy had brought up the main body of his attacking force? It is a curious tactic for a man committed to the defense of private property, and one that surely calls for explanation. The explanation is not far to seek, but it casts grave doubts on the zeal of the defender—already, as we have seen, not above suspicion.

The argument against community of property at the end of Book I is neither novel nor remarkable, but it is venerable and durable. It raises the two classical problems of egalitarian socialism: the problem of incentives and the problem of order and authority. Where rewards are not proportioned to effective effort, what will induce the worker to give his full share of energy to the common fund of necessary labor? And in a society of equals, whence arises the will to obey the ruling authorities, essential for the maintenance of public order and domestic concord?

[15] L 109-110, E 45, C 45

We need not seek to evaluate these arguments against egalitarianism and the community of property ourselves; we need only to try to learn how More evaluated them. To this end let us consider them in connection with Hythloday's discourse on the Utopian commonwealth. Now this commonwealth fulfilled precisely the conditions that according to the attack on community of property in Book I must lead to economic and social disaster. In Utopia regard for their own gains did *not* drive men to work, since there were no private gains to regard. All fruits of labor beyond those consumed by their producers went into the common store, and all the necessities of life were freely drawn from that store.[16] Consequently, of course, "no man can . . . defend that for his own which he hath gotten with the labor of his own hands." As to gradations of rank in Utopia, they were not utterly destroyed, but they were entirely based on election to office by popular vote,[17] and therefore they fell far below the minimum differentiation of status that respectable people of rank in the sixteenth century deemed essential for the preservation of a properly and decently ordered society. All Utopians have an equal opportunity for education,[18] all do equal labor,[19] and all have an equal voice in the choice of magistrates and priests.[20]

But what of the dire consequences that the argument in Book I against the community of property ascribes to such social arrangements? Is there no "abundance of goods or of anything"[21] in Utopia? On the contrary there is "store and abundance of all things that be requisite either for the neces-

[16] L 156-157, E 61, C 67-68 [17] L 135-136, E 54, C 57

[18] L 140-143, E 55-56, C 59-61

[19] L 139-148, E 55-58, C 59-63. The sole exception to this rule and the one concerning education is made for five hundred citizens out of the whole population, who devote themselves to learning. They are chosen on the basis of merit, and sent back to manual labor if they come short of what is expected of them. L 148, E 58, C 63

[20] L 135, 283; E 54, 105; C 57, 131 [21] L 105, E 45, C 45

sity or commodity of life."[22] Are the Utopians slothful, "everyman withdrawing his hand from labor"?[23] On the contrary no Utopian has "*victuals*[24] given him until he has . . . dispatched so much work as there is wont to be wrought before supper."[25] For the inhabitants of the Fortunate Isle there is indeed "little liberty . . . to loiter . . . no cloak or pretense to idleness."[26] Does the regime of equality in Utopia take away "the authority and reverence of magistrates"?[27] On the contrary the magistrates are there called fathers and "the citizens willingly exhibit unto them due honor without any compulsion."[28] And far from being prey to "continual sedition and bloodshed,"[29] Utopia is a land without "jeopardy of domestical dissension," where "perfect concord remaineth."[30] So the poverty, sloth, and disorder that the argument in Book I supposes to be the consequence of community of property do not exist in Utopia. Instead that land of community of property enjoys the abundance, industriousness, and harmonious order that are supposed to be, but are not, the fruit of the regime of private property.

Indeed it is the rather sour cream of the jest that it is not Utopia but sixteenth century Europe, with its well-rooted institutions of private property, that is running to ruin with scarcity, idleness, and crimes of violence. Such surely is the conclusion that More intends the reader to draw from the social criticism of the Europe of his day so brilliantly and wittily set out in both the Dialogue and the Discourse. And this contrast between Europe and Utopia is the consequence of no mere accident. It is the "form and fashion" of Utopian society, its "institutions of life," that have "laid such foundations of their commonwealth, as shall continue and last not

[22] L 145, E 57, C 62
[23] L 109, E 45, C 45
[24] "meat"; *cibus*
[25] L 168-169, E 65, C 74
[26] L 169, E 65, C 74
[27] L 110, E 45, C 45
[28] L 233, E 88, C 105
[29] L 110, E 45, C 45
[30] L 307, E 114, C 142-143

only wealthily, but also, as far as man's wit may judge and conjecture, shall endure forever."[31] Among those institutions of life not the least important is community of property. The Utopians live industriously, abundantly, and peacefully not in spite of the community of property practiced there, but in a very considerable measure because of it.

And now we can discern the function in the artistic economy of *Utopia* of the argument against the community of property that More ascribes to himself in Book I. It is revealed by Hythloday's immediate response to it: "You conceive in your mind either none at all, or else a very false image and similitude of this thing. But if you had been with me in Utopia and had presently seen their fashions and laws, as I did, . . . then doubtless you would grant that you never saw people well ordered, but only there."[32] More's argument serves to set the theme and provide the springboard for Hythloday's description of the Utopian commonwealth, and by the time he has finished describing it, he has not merely defended the community of property in general; he has specifically met all More's objections to it point by point. And this strongly suggests that More made the argument simply that it might be met point by point; that he was setting up a straw man just to have it knocked down. Yet even this does not do full justice to the artfulness of More's procedure when we call to mind that the Discourse which met the objections was written before the Dialogue in which they are raised. Thus he did not tailor the answers to fit the objections. In Through-the-Looking-Glass fashion he tailored the objections to fit the answers he already had given. He did not set up a straw man in order to knock it down; he actually set up a straw man that he had already not only knocked down but utterly and completely demolished.

The parts of *Utopia* that More wrote in England represent

[31] L 307, E 114, C 142

[32] L 110-111, E 45, C 45-46

his second thought only in the very literal sense that they deal in the main with a subject that he had not thought of writing about when he was in the Netherlands. But whenever the course of the added section overlaps that of the original version, the opinions expressed in both coincide exactly one with the other. The only difference in this respect between More's other opinions and his opinions on private property is that in the former case the overlapping is a casual result of the course of the argument he happens at the moment to be pursuing, while in the latter case it is clearly contrived. Only on the subject of property does More obviously go out of his way to use the part of *Utopia* written in England to reinforce a view expressed in the original version of *Utopia* written in the Netherlands. His second thought on the question of property was merely to reiterate and reaffirm his first thought.

3. THE ORTHODOX VIEW: WHAT MORE'S FRIENDS BELIEVED

At this point further to demonstrate the sincerity and seriousness of More's aversion to private property may seem supererogatory; but rather as a work of entertainment than as one of edification it may be pointed out that More had an opportunity for a third thought, and that if silence gives consent, as it certainly seems to do in this instance, More's third thought appears to be identical with his first and second.

More's opportunity for a third thought came at the time of the publication of the Basel edition of *Utopia* and in connection with literary contributions that three eminent humanists made to that edition. The contributions were the congratulatory letters of Jerome Busleyden[1] and Guillaume Budé,[2] the first addressed to More, the second to Lupset, who put the Paris edition of *Utopia* through the press; and the marginal

[1] L 313-319

[2] L lxxx-xcii

notes probably written by Erasmus.[3] The letter of Busleyden, Provost of Aire, Master of Requests to Archduke Charles, and founder of the famous College of Three Tongues at Louvain, appeared in the first edition of *Utopia*, published at Louvain, in September 1516, by Thierry Martens.[4] The marginal notes also appeared in this edition. In the unauthorized Paris edition that came out late in 1517 Busleyden's letter and the notes also were included along with the letter of Budé, the greatest of French classical scholars, whose persistent efforts, beginning in that very year, were to bring about the establishment of a French academy of the New Learning, the Collège de France. And so we have in these three documents interpretations of *Utopia* by a highly select group of More's contemporaries—all in close rapport with his intellectual ideals, two the most eminent literati in Europe, one who had been much with him while he was working out the original version of *Utopia*,[5] and one his dearest friend. In view of the divergent interpretations of later centuries, these three men were remarkably in accord as to the intent of the author, especially with respect to his social ideas.

From reading *Utopia*, says Budé, "I perceive that all the theory and practice of domestic economy, all care whatever for increasing one's income, was mere waste of time. And yet, as all see and are aware, the whole race of mankind is goaded on by this very thing, as if some gadfly were bred within them to sting them. The result is that we needs must confess

[3] L passim. There is some doubt as to whether the marginal notes are by Erasmus or Peter Giles. My preference for Erasmus is based on the enthusiasm the commentator displays for every jibe More makes at the monastic orders—e.g., L 73-77. Erasmus' antipathy to the order priests is too well known to require documentation here. In 1516, with his case for a dispensation from fulfillment of his monastic vows coming up in Rome, his feelings on the subject were doubtless intensified.

[4] The details of the contents and dates of publication of the Louvain, Paris, and Basel editions will be found in L lxiv-lxxvi.

[5] N 2:260-261; A 2:388, lines 140-147

the object of nearly all civil and legal training and discipline to be this: that with jealous and watchful cunning, as each one has a neighbor with whom he is connected by ties of citizenship, or even at times of kinship, he should ever be conveying or abstracting something from him; should pare away, repudiate, squeeze, chouse, chisel, cozen, extort, pillage, purloin, thieve, filch, rob, and—partly with the connivance, partly with the sanction of the laws—be ever plundering and appropriating. . . . But the founder and regulator of all property, Jesus Christ, left among His followers a Pythagorean community and love. . . . Utopia . . . is said . . . to have adopted Christian usages; . . . to have imbibed the wisdom thereto belonging; and to have kept it undefiled to this very day. . . . It holds with firm grip to three divine institutions—absolute equality . . . in all things good and evil among citizens, a settled and unwavering love of peace and quietness, and a contempt for gold and silver. . . . Would that God in His goodness had dealt so kindly with the countries which . . . are known by His Most Holy Name! Surely then greed which perverts and sinks down so many minds, otherwise noble and elevated, would depart thence once and for all, and the golden age of Saturn would return."[6]

In the same sense, according to Busleyden, "All must long for the right and good constitution of the Utopian commonwealth . . . an ideal commonwealth, a pattern and finished model of conduct, than which there has never been seen in the world one more wholesome in its institution, or more perfect, or to be thought more desirable. . . . No wonder . . . it comes . . . as an object of . . . reverence to all nations, and one for all generations to tell of; the more so that in it all competition for ownership is taken away, and no one has any private property at all. For the rest all men have all things in common, with a view to the commonwealth itself; so that

[6] L lxxxii-lxxxiii, lxxxvi, lxxxvii, lxxxviii-lxxxix

every matter, every action, however unimportant, whether public or private, instead of being directed to the greed of the many or the caprice of the few, has sole reference to the upholding of one uniform justice, equality, and communion. When that is made the entire object of every action, there must needs be a clearing away of all that serves as matter and fuel to feed intrigue, of luxury, envy and wrong, to which men are hurried on . . . either by the possession of private property, or by the burning thirst of gain, and that most pitiable of all things, ambition, to their own great and immeasurable loss. For it is from these things that there often suddenly arise divisions of feeling, taking up of arms, and wars worse than civil, whereby the flourishing state of wealthy commonwealths is often overthrown."[7]

Such were the interpretations Budé and Busleyden put on the social intent of the author of *Utopia.* The interpretation of Erasmus in the nature of the case is not so coherently stated. His marginal comments, rarely more than two or three words, are usually neutral and banal. A few, however, express the sentiments of their author, and a very few indicate his interpretation of More's remarks on the use of money, private property, and the Utopian community of property. He is delighted by the story of the Anemolian ambassadors: "a most elegant tale";[8] and by the base uses to which the Utopians put the noble metals: "O, magnificent contempt for gold!"[9] He approves of the common Utopian obligation to farm labor,[10] and of Utopian abolition of the luxuries that are the marks of status in Europe.[11] He notes how much the Utopians are able to achieve through mutual labor,[12] and says that it is because of the equality of things in Utopia that there is enough for everybody.[13] He calls particular attention to the description of European commonwealths as conspiracies of

[7] L 314, 315, 316-317 [8] L 177 [9] L 175
[10] L 139 [11] L 146 [12] L 118, 125 [13] L 169

the rich with a "Note this, reader!"[14] When More ascribes to pride Europe's failure to adopt Utopian institutions Erasmus calls it a "wonderful saying."[15] For him, Utopia is a "holy commonwealth that Christians ought to imitate."[16]

And so neither Budé, nor Busleyden, nor Erasmus looked upon the social ideas More set down in the *Utopia* as a mere cultivated joke; they did not doubt his underlying seriousness; and they certainly did not think he was defending the excellence of private property against the assaults of Hythloday. They thought he was praising community of property and rejecting private property as the basis of the Good Society. Now it is possible that Busleyden's letter and Erasmus' notes were put in the Louvain edition without More's consent, and it is probable that not only the Budé letter but the whole Paris edition was published without More's knowledge. Up to the second edition, then, we cannot infer too much from the presence of those documents in *Utopia*. This, however, is not the case with respect to the edition that Froben printed in the spring of 1518. Erasmus had asked More for corrections to the first edition a year previously with a view to a new printing at Basel.[17] In March 1518, he explained to More that Froben had delayed going to press until he received Budé's "elegant preface."[18] So More certainly knew what was in the marginal notes and in Busleyden's letter by the time the Basel edition was being made ready;[19] and he probably knew the contents of Budé's letter, too. And he knew that all three would appear in the new edition. Now if present-day scholars who see a defense of private property in *Utopia* are right, then Erasmus, Busleyden, and Budé are wrong in their interpretation of More's intent. And if More

[14] L 303 [15] L 306 [16] L 169
[17] N 2:514; A 2:543, lines 11-13 [18] N 3:289; A 3:785, lines 14-16
[19] Already in January 1517 More had written Busleyden to thank him for his prefatory letter to *Utopia*; N 2:455; A 2:513, lines 6-8.

allowed the marginal notes and letters to appear in the Basel edition without corrections at the appropriate points, he was certainly lending a measure of confirmation and official status to that error. Correction in the case of the marginal notes would have been especially easy. All More needed to do was to erase a half dozen of them and transfer the *mire dictum* from Hythloday's excoriation of the pride of Christians in clinging to private property to his own excoriation of community of property. It is quite clear that he did no such thing. And so we are left with two alternatives. Either More was willing to see what was bound to be construed as the stamp of his approval placed on a complete misinterpretation of his ideas; or there was no misinterpretation, his friends understood his intent quite well, and his third thought was what his first and second had been. As between these two alternatives I do not find it very difficult to choose.

4. UTOPIAN PHILOSOPHY AND THEOLOGY

Some recent writers who do not seek to make More's views on private property vanish altogether nevertheless tend to minimize the importance of those views for the general significance of *Utopia.* Authors in "the hagiographic tradition of More scholarship"[1] have achieved this end by suggesting that More's encomium of community of property and goods was a manifestation of More's conservatism and medievalism against the onrush of capitalist aggression, essentially a defense of the monastic orders—those "rightest Christian companies," which practiced community of property and goods—against the greedy, grasping hands of the rising middle class.[2] Having tidied up this little point, which we will have to untidy again later, writers in the hagiographic tradition either dismiss *Utopia* as one of More's lesser works

[1] Ames, p. 105.
[2] R. W. Chambers, *Thomas More,* New York, 1936, pp. 131-138.

with no serious intent[3] or concentrate their attention on the sections dealing with Utopian philosophy and religion almost to the exclusion of those on Utopian social and economic policy. The contention that *Utopia* is a minor work of More is too silly to waste time on, involving as it does an estimate of the book shared neither by More's contemporaries nor by posterity for the past four hundred years.[4] The height of achievement along the second line of treatment of *Utopia* is an essay—and within its limitations a very good essay—on "Designs by Erasmus and More for a New Social Order" that derives More's philosophy and his social theory from late classical Stoicism, and that from beginning to end does not directly mention his democratic egalitarianism or his attack on private property at all.[5]

Yet to regard the sections on religion and philosophy[6] as the key to the interpretation of *Utopia* and to the intent of its author is in effect to surrender at the outset any hope of determining what that intent was. There are parts of *Utopia* a careful and close examination of which may reveal beyond reasonable doubt the intent of their author, but no amount of examination, however close and careful, of the sections on Utopian philosophy and religion can render us certain to what extent the opinions there expressed are More's own. This unresolvable uncertainty is a consequence of the literary form into which More cast *Utopia*. That form is the traveler's

[3] Claude Jenkins, *Sir Thomas More*, Canterbury, 1935, pp. 19-20, "What More has done is amuse himself with a phantasy after the ancient model . . . a genial satire . . . it is a learned diversion of a learned world . . . and one which More's own Cardinal Morton . . . would have allowed in jest."

[4] The chronology of editions and translations of *Utopia* spread through thirteen pages of the More bibliography provide an adequate measure of contemporary and later judgment of the book. Sullivan, sub. *Utopia*.

[5] Robert Adams, "Designs by Erasmus and More for a New Social Order," *Studies in Philology*, 42, 1945, pp. 131-145.

[6] L 183-211, 266-298; E 71-80, 100-110; C 81-94, 123-138

tale; the "best state of the commonwealth" is described as a real land existing somewhere on the other side of the earth in More's own time. Now because the *Republic* was by definition a purely imaginative construction, Plato could furnish it with any customs, laws, and institutions that suited his taste; but because of his literary apparatus More could only ascribe to the Utopians such customs, laws, and institutions as conceivably might prevail on the other side of the world in his own day. As to secular institutions that was latitude enough, a *carte blanche* indeed. But in religion it was otherwise; Utopia, the best state of the commonwealth, could not be Christian since it lay in a region of the world where the light of the Christian Gospel had never shone.

More nevertheless takes considerable pains by means of two devices to draw the Utopian commonwealth as near to Christianity as his literary form will let him. In the first place, when the Utopians "heard us speak of the name of Christ, of His doctrine, laws, miracles . . . you will not believe with how glad minds they agreed unto the same. . . . This was no small help and furtherance in the matter that they heard us say that *a community of living among His followers was pleasing to Christ*,[7] and that the same community doth yet remain among the rightest Christian companies."[8] The suggestion seems to be that the Utopians were brought to such a degree of natural perfection by their social institutions that as soon as they heard Christian truth expounded they were ready to receive it. In the second place, More provided the Utopians with a philosophy that was as close to Christianity as men could get by the exercise of natural reason.[9] As the writer

[7] "Christ instituted among His all things common"; *Christo communem suorum victum . . . placuisse.*

[8] L 268-269, E 100-101, C 124

[9] L 211, E 80, C 94. Robinson has More say that "in that part of philosophy which intreateth of matters and virtues their reasons and opinions agree with ours," L 187, E 72, C 83. This is a mistranslation of the main clause,

referred to above has indicated, this philosophy has affinities with late Roman Stoicism, which is intelligible enough, since in this matter More is in a sense recapitulating, in a sense reversing, the historical development of the Christian faith itself. That faith was chiliastic in the minds of its early adherents, and therefore it did not at first develop any considerable coherent social doctrine. When the anticipated Last Day failed to arrive, Christian believers had to be provided with a social ethic to cope with life in this world. At that point, because of their congeniality with the general Christian world view, large chunks of Stoic social doctrine were incorporated into the body of Christian thought.[10] It is little wonder, then, that when More had to strip off the revealed elements of Christianity in order to provide the Utopians with a philosophic and religious ethic the result had affinities with later Stoicism, familiar to him through the writings of Cicero and Seneca and already partly assimilated into Christian ethical tradition.

More's reconstruction of a philosophy and a religion for his Utopians based on natural reason, and attaining what was probably to his mind the highest perfection that natural reason could reach,[11] is a neat *tour de force*; but because it is a *tour de force* imposed on More by the literary mould of *Utopia*, it is not a sure guide to his own philosophical and religious views. This mould, by placing Utopia beyond the range of Christendom, forced him to endow the best state of the com-

---

eadem illis disputantur quae nobis, which means "They argue about—or have disputations on—the same *things* as we do." Robinson's error might lead the reader to a considerable overestimate of the extent of More's commitment to the ethical view which he proceeds to describe.

[10] In this analysis I follow Ernst Troeltsch, *The Social Teaching of the Christian Churches,* 1 vol. in 2, tr. O. Wyon, New York, 1931, pp. 64-68.

[11] "This is their sentence and opinion of vertue and pleasure. And they believe that by man's reason none can be found truer than this," L 210-211, E 80, C 94

monwealth with what from his point of view could only be a second-best philosophy and religion. Natural reason could not possibly attain to the best religion and the best philosophy,[12] because for More that best religion was Christianity, and that best philosophy was "the philosophy of Christ." Thomas More was a Christian humanist.

This is not the place to enter into the details of the long controversy over the nature, origin, and history of Christian humanism; but my classification of More's intellectual position as Christian humanist obliges me briefly to describe and defend the rubric. This description of Christian humanism can and should be kept clear of arguments about whether the Renaissance was Christian or pagan, and even of arguments about whether there was really a Renaissance at all. However one distributes the labels and the honorific and imprecatory designations, from the fourteenth century on there existed a group of men, first in Italy and later in the rest of Catholic Christendom, profoundly preoccupied with the restoration and propagation of *bonae literae*, the writings of antiquity, first Latin then Greek. With few exceptions these men of letters believed that the study of the literary works of antiquity revealed a culture not only of more refined taste than their own but of superior moral values and standards for the conduct of life; and so, vocationally for some and avocationally for others, the education of Europe in these values and standards became a part of their life work. These men are called humanists, and with few if any exceptions they were Christians of one sort or another. But a humanist who was a Christian was not necessarily a Christian humanist in the sense intended above. In that sense not even humanists who believed that education in *bonae literae* would make particu-

[12] Rather cleverly More has the Utopians themselves allow for this possibility by completing the sentence quoted in note 11 ". . . unless any godlier be inspired into man from Heaven."

lar men better Christians were Christian humanists. Two essential traits, inseparable and interrelated, distinguished the Christian humanists. They were as ardently devoted to the literature of Christian antiquity—the early Fathers and the New Testament—as to the literature of pagan antiquity; and they passionately believed that embedded in both those literatures was a wisdom that could both improve individual men and, far more important, renovate the moribund Christian society of their own day temporally and spiritually, in head and members. It was the conviction that they had a universal saving Christian mission that imbued with an evangelical fervor even the more abstruse scholarly enterprises of the Christian humanists, such as Erasmus' editorial labors on the epistles of St. Jerome. The ultimate fruit for life of their conviction and fervor was the "philosophy of Christ," which without a distinctive physics, metaphysics, cosmology, esthetics, epistemology, or logic was not in a technical sense a philosophy at all. While abundantly learned it was anti-intellectual to the extent that it was hostile to the intellectualism represented by the theological and philosophic tradition of the European universities. It was also anti-intellectual in appealing from subtle ratiocination to common sense and most emphatically from the head to the heart. Christian humanism was thus not so much an integrated edifice of ideas as a program of action, a propaganda, and the Christian humanists were not so much like-minded with respect to the details of theological and philosophic doctrine as they were like-hearted in their hopes of social and spiritual renewal through a restoration of Gospel Christianity.

The objectives of Eramus already formulated in 1501 in the *Enchiridion Militis Christiani* may stand for those of his ramifying circle of friends, including Thomas More: "To lead men back to Christ—that became the task of theology. The antagonism of esthetic taste and classical culture to scholasticism was permeated by an ethical and religious revulsion from a theology that through its union with logic had lost its connection with the vital sources of living piety. To base himself on the Gospels, to distinguish between the divine and the human in living and learning, once again to set forth the philosophy of Christ in its purity formed the true content of Erasmus' life work. The purity and simplicity of the Gospel became his highest ideal and norm for living as well as for learning. On this foundation Erasmus sought to mould Western society in an enlightened humanist direction, 'to shape the *Res Publica Christiana* in its threefold manifestation as hierarchy, sacramental instrument of salvation, and organic system, into a community of culture. Then from the hierarchy would develop a school of Christ, from the sacramental instrument of salvation a Christian fellowship, and from the organic system, a philosophic morality resting on a *consensus opinionum* concerning the ideals of Christian brotherhood.' "[13]

Two essential elements of Christian humanism bear on the question of the relation of Utopian religion and philosophy to Thomas More's own opinions. In the first place like other Christian humanists More believed that the gentile writers of antiquity had arrived at certain profound moral and perhaps even religious truths. But he also believed that the ultimate truths, religious and moral alike, were fully revealed only in the New Testament, that without the light of Revelation the whole truth can be glimpsed but partially, through a glass very darkly indeed. Now as we have said, More probably intended Utopian philosophy and religion to represent the nearest approach natural reason can make to Christian truth. The trouble is that *in any particular matter* we have no way

[13] Otto Schottenloher, *Erasmus im Ringen um die Humanistische Bildungsform*, Reformationsgeschichtliche Studien und Texte, 61, 1933, p. 113.

of telling how near he believed natural reason came to Christian truth or how far he believed it fell short of it. We cannot measure the deviation by setting the natural philosophy and religion of the Utopians against Church philosophy, practice, and policy in More's time. Much of the teaching, practice, and policy of the Church in his day was to More's mind further from the philosophy of Christ than the ideas of the ancient gentile moralists were. How this curious situation affects our capacity to deduce More's philosophic and religious ideas from those ascribed to the Utopians will be nicely illustrated if we examine More's description of Utopian policy in religious matters.[14] That policy was, according to one's taste in epithet, very liberal or very lax. Anyone professing belief in God and a future life of rewards and punishments was free both to hold and to propagate his particular doctrine if he did so without rancor or violence.[15] Even men who denied God and immortality, though deemed unfit for citizenship, were not deprived of life or livelihood, or even forbidden to discuss their opinions as long as they directed their discussion only to learned men and did not seek to subvert the multitude.[16] Such a method of dealing with religious difference is a far cry from the capricious but violent policy of the Church in More's day with its hasty and harsh punishments of deviations from orthodoxy. As between Utopian toleration, dictated by natural reason and Catholic heresy hunting dictated by the Inquisition and the orthodox princes, what was More's position? Did he believe that Christian truth called for the same measure of toleration as natural reason did? Perhaps; scarcely half a century later there were very pious Christians who held that religious toleration was the Gospel rule, and that the role of persecutor was death to the Faith. Did he approve of the terrible punishment that the ruling

[14] L 270-276, E 101-103, C 125-127
[15] L 271-274, E 101-103, C 125-127
[16] L 274-276, E 102-103, C 127

powers of his day inflicted on religious deviation? Again perhaps; later in his life he certainly championed the suppression of heretics by force; but these heretics propagated their faith with a great deal of "violence . . . and seditious words . . . vehemently and fervently."[17] And for such as these even the mild law of Utopia decreed banishment or bondage.[18] And so we have no notion what relation Utopian religious policy bore to More's opinion of the correct religious policy of a Christian commonwealth. And what is true of religious policy is true of almost everything else in the sections on philosophy and religion in *Utopia.* A reconstruction of More's own opinions based on those sections has shaky foundations.

If the sector of thought covered in the chapters on Utopian philosophy and religion was—as it has sometimes been treated—the key to More's meaning in the whole of *Utopia* or in the *Utopia* of his first intention, we would have on our hands a work so contrived by the author that its central ideas were bound to elude the reader's grasp. But in fact the Utopian philosophy and religion are peripheral to the main themes of the work. I do not mean to suggest that religion and general philosophy were unimportant to More. But every book a man writes need not deal fully and precisely with all matters that he deems important, and as we have seen the very form of the Utopian Discourse disqualifies it from the outset as a vehicle for the clear and decisive expression of More's own religious and philosophical views.

5. PLANNING IN THE GOOD SOCIETY

More himself must have been quite aware of this, and yet he felt impelled to include in his book a section on Utopian philosophy and religion. The intellectual impulsion that thrust him into this undertaking remains highly significant. He had

[17] L 272, E 102, C 126 [18] *ibid.*

to provide Utopia with a religion and philosophy worthy of it, and the religion and philosophy worthy of it were the best possible ones within the limits that his literary problem imposed on him. They had to be the best possible philosophy and religion because More truly believed that the Utopian commonwealth as he had framed it was the Best Society. That he did indeed believe this he indicates time after time, but never more emphatically than at the beginning of the summation with which he closed the original version of *Utopia*: "Now I have declared and described to you, as truly as I could, the form and order of that commonwealth which verily in my judgment is not only the best, but also that which alone of good right may claim and take upon it the name of a commonwealth or public weal."[1]

Just as emphatically this summation tells us what More believed to be the very root and foundation of that Best Society. It is not the religion of the Utopians nor their philosophy. It is not even their egalitarian political democracy, which on closer inspection turns out to be not so egalitarian after all.[2] He has spoken of all these things and many more in the Utopian Discourse, but not once does he revert to them in Hythloday's peroration. What makes Utopia the Best Society is explicitly the abolition of a money economy, of private property, and of the institutional pattern of which they were a part: "In other places they speak still of the commonwealth. But every man procureth his own private wealth. Here where nothing is private the common affairs be earnestly looked upon."[3] Or, as More says in that last feeble defense of private property which he put into his own mouth,

[1] L 299, E 110-111, C 138

[2] The highest offices in Utopia go only to a specially educated intellectual élite; but of course compared with the common, rigidly hierarchical ideology of More's day, this reservation occurs far down the road to egalitarianism. L 148, E 58, C 63

[3] L 299, E 111, C 138

"Their common life and community of living without any traffic in money . . . is the ultimate foundation of all their institutions."[4] Or again, "Where possessions be private, where money beareth all the stroke, it is hard and almost impossible that there the weal public may justly be governed and prosperously flourish."[5] So More believed in the community of property and goods, and with him it was no peripheral or casual belief; in the literal sense of the word it was fundamental. The abolition of private property and money was an essential element in the very foundation of the Good Society.

Although his theory of property stands at the center of More's argument, we shall not understand his intent in *Utopia* until we consider that theory in conjunction with three other essential facts about More's conceptions and way of thinking revealed by the original version of that work:

(1) More did not believe that men were so hopelessly corrupt as to be forever incapable of a decent social order. Or, to state the same thing positively, More did believe human nature to be sufficiently malleable so that under the proper external—Marx might have said objective—conditions it was capable of attaining to the Good Society.

(2) More's approach to the problem of the conditions necessary for a Good Society is not the direct one of seeking the nature of perfect justice and deducing therefrom the political and social institutions requisite for its attainment. His approach is indirect. He investigates the social evils of his own time until he discovers what he believes to be their roots, and then he systematically elaborates the regimen necessary to eradicate those evils.

(3) Although in his book More displays immense skill at devising specific and practical methods to attain envisaged

[4] L 308, E 114, C 143. For translation see Part Two, section 2, note 1.
[5] L 104-105, E 43, C 43

ends within the Utopian commonwealth (as a planner More is way out in front of Plato and Marx), on one problem—the most practical of all—he has nothing whatever to say. He offers no suggestion on how the corrupt Christian commonwealth, whose rottenness his probings into the social disorders of his time lays bare, can be transformed into the Good Society. Here the man of expedients proposes no expedients, the man of method no methods; here there is only silence. His very last words in the published version of *Utopia* point to the abyss that he had left in the original version: "Many things be in the Utopian weal public which in our cities I may rather wish for than hope after."[6] The words point to the abyss; they do nothing to bridge it.

Let us consider these points one by one.

The Utopians are "natural men" in that they live by and their institutions are founded upon that natural law which is reason; but they are not unfallen men, innocent of evil, or perfect men, incapable of evil.[7] In the original version of *Utopia* More does not put himself in the position of the totally irresponsible idealist, who says in effect, "Thus it would be if all men were truly good, but since they are not good and never will be, nothing I say need be taken to heart." Utopia is the best of commonwealths, and Utopians are the best of men; but it is not because they are of a better stuff and nature than other men; it is because their laws, ordinances, rearing, and rules of living are such as to make effective man's natural capacity for good, while suppressing his natural propensity for evil.[8] The sound social, political, and economic

[6] L 309, E 115, C 144

[7] There are Utopians ". . . who could not . . . be refrained (restrained) from misdoing," L 222, E 83, C 99

[8] "These and such like opinions have they conceived, partly by education, being brought up in that commonwealth, whose laws and customs be far different from these kinds of folly and partly by good literature and learning," L 183, E 71, C 81

regimen under which they live is the cause of the civic virtue of the Utopians, not the other way about; their institutions are not the creation but the creator of their good qualities. The mere absence of money in the Utopian economy preserves the Utopians from a veritable plague of sins and crimes. "*When money itself ceases to be useful, all greed for it is also entirely submerged; then what a heap of troubles is leveled down, what a crop of enormities is pulled up by the roots.*[9] For who knoweth not that fraud, theft, ravine, brawling, quarreling, brabbling, strife, chiding, contention, murder, treason, poisoning, which by the *usual*[10] punishments are rather revenged than refrained do die when money dieth? And also that fear, grief, care, distress, and anxiety do perish even at the very same moment that money perisheth?"[11] And thus it is in Utopia. The Utopians thus refrain from this whole array of misdeeds and escape this whole net of evils, not because they are naturally better than other men, but because their fundamental law—their *police*, to use a contemporary French equivalent—destroys not merely money itself, but the very utility of money.

In the methodical and complete annihilation of the foundations of a money economy in Utopia More achieves a true masterpiece of constructive imagination. Examine the structure of Utopian society as closely and as often as you wish, you will not find a place in it where the possession of money could possibly do anyone the slightest good. While the pressure for diligent labor is carefully maintained, every incentive to accumulation and acquisitiveness is systematically destroyed. For example, in a pecuniary society two of the prime uses of

[9] "how great an occasion of wickedness and mischief is plucked up by the roots?" *cum ipso usu sublata penitus omni auiditate pecuniae, quanta moles molestiarium recisa, quanta scelerum seges radicitus euulsa est?*

[10] "daily"; *cotidianis*

[11] L 304, E 113, C 141

money are to purchase immunity from labor and to acquire the paraphernalia of invidious distinction—more luxurious living quarters and finer clothing, among others. But since in Utopia those who did not work did not eat,[12] and vagrant spirits who sought to evade the law of labor were made bondmen,[13] immunity from toil could not be bought with money or otherwise. Money, moreover, could not purchase the badges of invidious distinction in a society where education was universal and free, where the common table was the best table,[14] where dwellings were not privately owned,[15] and where clothing was both abundant, and uniform and plain in color and quality.[16] Even the more amiable motives for acquisitiveness in a pecuniary society—solicitude for the future welfare of one's self and one's family—evaporate in a commonwealth that makes adequate provision for all but permits no richer provision for one than for another. The Utopians are consequently free of all the anxiety and all the resultant hostile emulation with which men in a pecuniary society are oppressed and with which they oppress one another. "*For what can be more rich than to live joyfully and tranquilly without any worry, not fearful for his own livlihood, nor vexed and troubled with his wife's importunate complaints, not dreading poverty to his sons, nor anxious about his daughter's dowry? But instead to be secure about the livelihood and happiness of their wives, children, grandchildren, and their posterity which they handsomely assume will be a long line.*"[17] After patiently blocking off every other possible

[12] L 168-169, E 65, C 74 [13] L 168, E 65, C 73 [14] L 161, E 63, C 70
[15] L 130, E 53, C 55 [16] L 150-151, E 59, C 64-65

[17] "For what can be more rich than to live joyfully and merrily, without all grief and pensiveness; not caring for his own living, nor vexed or troubled with his wife's importunate complaints, not dreading poverty to his son, nor sorrowing for his daughter's dowry? Yea, they take no care at all for the living and wealth of themselves and all theirs; of their wives, their children, their nephews, their children's children, and all the suces-

use for gold in Utopia, More rewards his own labor of love with a well-earned and triumphant joke. In Utopia's internal economy gold is used for the only purposes he has left for it; it is employed in the manufacture of chains for slaves and of chamber pots for citizens.[18]

6. MORE AS A REALIST

Because quite a few present-day academic prestidigitators have felt impelled to make More's conception of the community of property and goods, recently become politically embarrassing, softly and silently vanish away and never be heard of again, I have felt justified in taking special pains to indicate the central importance of that conception in *Utopia*. But it is unjust to More and to the scope of his conceptions to summarize and dismiss the Utopian social economy with the bare flat phrase: community of property and goods. For in the bare idea there was nothing new in More's time or long before. There were a number of variations on the idea both in theory and in practice available in More's day and well within the bounds of his knowledge. On the theoretical side he was familiar with Plato's *Republic*, with Seneca, and with the great Latin Fathers; on the practical side he knew about the way of life of the early Christian groups and especially about the prescriptions of the Benedictine Rule.

More's originality then—and he was one of the very few original social thinkers in the two centuries before Calvin—

sion that ever shall follow in their posterity"; *Nam quid ditius esse potest, quam, edempta prorsus omni solicitudine, laeto ac tranquilo animo uiuere? non de suo uicta trepidum, non uxoris querula flagitatione uexatum, non paupertatum filio metuentem, non de filiae dote anxium; sed de suo suorumque omnium, uxoris, filiorum, nepotum, pronepotum, abnepotum, et quam longam posterorum seriem generosi praesumunt, uictu esse ac felicitate securum,* L 300, E 111, C 139

[18] L 175-176, E 68, C 77

lay not in the bare idea of a community of property and goods; it lay in the exactness, the precision, and the meticulous detail with which he implemented his underlying social conceptions, proposing all the basic rules of law and methods of administration necessary to make community of property and goods one of the motor forces in a going polity. But his achievement in this matter rests on a prior feat of the mind. For More proceeds to his Utopian—in some ways even Draconian—remedies only after he has made a careful diagnosis of the evils of society, and not of society in the general and abstract sense, but of sixteenth century Christendom as it lay before his sharp probing eyes.

Both in the detailed penetrating diagnosis of contemporary ills and in the detailed prescription of requisite remedies, More surpassed the usual limits and limitations of traditional social satire and of humanist social criticism. His beloved Erasmus both amalgamates the satire with the social criticism and in his own work reveals their shortcomings. The corruption of the papal curia, the follies and frivolities of the courts of princes and the vainglory of the princes themselves, the chicanery of men of law, the idleness and laziness of monks, the pretensions and ignorance of the great—these targets of the shafts in the Erasmian armory had been shot at and shot at again by earlier satirists, some good-humored and mild, some angry and violent, ever since the twelfth century. The English tradition in this literary line runs from John of Salisbury and Walter Mapes through the Song of Lewes and the preaching friars to Langland, Chaucer, and at the very end of the Middle Ages, Thomas Gascoigne. To the ancient and traditional social criticism and satire Erasmus imparted a high literary polish, and that is about all. His partial abandonment of the hierarchical framework on which that criticism had been hung, though probably not altogether conscious, is interesting; but it leaves his own efforts incoherent and invertebrate, lacking in the structural form which that framework provided for the writings of his predecessors. *The Praise of Folly, The Complaint of Peace*, and the long satirical adages are inadequate as social criticism because they point to the sickness of early sixteenth century Christendom but scarcely ever penetrate inward to discover the roots of the disease. Therefore their prescriptions, in the rare instances when anything so specific is suggested, are mere analgesics and plasters, not radical remedies.

This criticism of Erasmus in no way applies to More. In his capacity to see past the symptoms to the sources of trouble, in his grasp of the intricacy and ramification of social structure and social action, in his skill at working out expedients to meet particular social problems—in short, in what is usually summed up under the rubric, Realism—More is not in the humanist tradition at all. In these matters he finds his intellectual kin among a small group of writers of his own time and a little earlier. These men both wrote about politics and actively engaged in the management of affairs of state at a high level; they were statesman-writers indeed: Sir John Fortescue, Lord Chief Justice of England, Philippe de Commynes and Claude Seyssel, one diplomat and advisor to Louis XI, the other to Louis XII, and Niccolò Machiavelli, secretary to the Florentine Republic.[1] Differing widely from one another in purposes and ideals, and exercising little or no reciprocal influence one on the other, they independently express and have in common the vivid and profound sense of political realities that is one of the most significant traits of the age of the New Monarchies in Europe. In sharing this

[1] Sir John Fortescue, *The Governance of England*, ed. C. Plummer, Oxford, 1885; Philippe de Commynes, *Mémoires*, 3 vols., ed. Calmette, Paris, 1924-1925; Claude Seyssel, passim; Niccolò Machiavelli, *Tutte le opere*, ed. G. Mazzoni and M. Casella, Florence, 1929.

sense and in his ability to articulate it, More is one with them.

This brings us to, in part indeed is, our second point. The community of property and goods, as set forth in the Discourse section of *Utopia,* is not the culmination of an abstract consideration of the nature of justice; it is one ingredient of a remedy which, if taken, would according to More eradicate most of the social evils of his own time. More's starting point is not a quest for what would be ideally right in the world but a good working idea of what was actually wrong with it. I do not wish to deal here in itemized detail with the particulars of what More thought was wrong with his world. That has been done often enough before, never quite so well as More did it himself in *Utopia,* where it is still easily available to be read. Although we shall have to give a little attention to some of those particulars later, here I want to try to push past the detail in order to determine what More believed sustained the rank garden of ills that he saw all around him. This is a somewhat more arduous task.

More was not of course the first to discover the sicknesses of sixteenth century society with which so much of both parts of *Utopia* are concerned, nor was he the first to draw attention to their existence. Most of the particular evils that he concerned himself with were conspicuous enough to attract the unfavorable attention of almost anyone who was not directly profiting from them. They had attracted such attention before *Utopia* was written. Further than that, item by item, and piecemeal, they had become the objects of Parliamentary legislation, royal administrative action, and local regulation. When More wrote of enclosure, vagabondage, the unemployed discharged soldier, the law's delays, the liveried bands of retainers, the recurrent straits of the cloth industry, and the engrossing and forestalling of produce to enhance its market price, he was considering problems of which for a quarter of a century in all cases, for more than a century in some, his compatriots had been well aware. His achievement lay not in discovering these evils in detail but in dealing with them as a related whole, not as individual plants but as growths which however separate they might appear on the surface had a concealed common root.

7. MORE AND MODERN SOCIALISM

At a first approximation it is clear that More found a common bond among the particular social ills of his time in the organization of society itself, especially in its economic aspect. It is equally clear that much of his prescription for those ills, both for their palliation in part I and for their cure in part II of *Utopia*, is of a kind usually called economic, and that the curative prescription contains three important ingredients—the community of property, the abolition of private profit, and the universal obligation to labor—which are today generally associated with socialism. Thus Karl Kautsky was led to observe that "More thought along modern lines, . . . his socialism was of a modern kind," and "More's . . . ideal . . . may be regarded as a foregleam of Modern Socialism."[1]

There can be no serious objection to describing the Utopian economy as socialist, but to ascribe to More a modern kind of socialism implies that he finds the ultimate explanation of the evils of his day in the mode of production and expects that those evils and all others will be cured by the establishment, and through the effect, of social control of the means of production.

Yet when he comes to make a closer examination of the Utopian economy, Kautsky has to confess that while "More's communism is modern in most of its tendencies" it is "unmodern in most of its expedients."[2] Its "unmodern" expedi-

[1] Kautsky, p. 171.   [2] *ibid.*, p. 214.

ents are the attachment of men to specific handicrafts,[3] the institution of compulsory bond labor,[4] and "the frugality of the Utopians," the "restriction of wants" in Utopia.[5] Kautsky has a modern socialist explanation for "these reactionary features" of *Utopia.* "The unmodern aspects of More's Communism are the necessary consequences of the mode of production he was obliged to take as his starting-point."[6] In a sense Kautsky is compelled to argue in this way. If the "reactionary features" are not casual, not merely imposed by the exigencies of a backward technology, but are of a piece with the other economic institutions of Utopia, then "the best state of the commonwealth" may still in a sense be socialist or communist; but a man who indifferently accepts or intentionally includes the handicraft system, compulsory labor and the restriction of wants in his ideal society is not a modern socialist. If More was a modern socialist, Kautsky seems to argue, given sixteenth century conditions he *might* still have had to fall back on reactionary measures; and since he *was* a modern socialist and *did* fall back on reactionary measures, he must have been constrained to do so by the conditions of his time. The argument simply assumes what it should prove and goes on from there. This may indeed be the best way to handle the problem, since of the constraint exercised on More's social ideal by the backwardness of early sixteenth century technology there is no evidence whatsoever.

The idea of labor-saving had not taken deep roots in the early sixteenth century. Little thought was given to the subject either on economic or humanitarian grounds; and it is a remarkable instance of More's gift for glimpsing ideals and aspirations scarcely even inchoate in his own day that he ascribes to the Utopians the virtue of being "marvelous quick in the invention of *skills which make in any way for the*

[3] *ibid.,* p. 206.
[4] *ibid.,* p. 208.
[5] *ibid.,* p. 209.
[6] *ibid.,* p. 206.

advantages of an abundant life."[7] Yet More certainly did not take the view common to all present-day social thought that maximum leisure and minimum labor as such are proper goals of economic organization. True the Utopian economy eliminated the back-breaking toil that in Europe reduced men to beasts of burden, and it permitted a kind of leisure to all who wished to enjoy it. But it was not leisure as such and at random but a very special kind of leisure that More valued. Time not spent in labor "they be suffered to bestow every man as he liketh best himself," says More, but the freedom held forth in this sentence is withdrawn in the very next: "Not to the intent that they should misspend this time in riot or slothfulness; but being then licensed from the labor of their own occupations, to bestow the time well and thriftily upon some other good science as shall please them." Utopians not inclined to spend their spare time in a relentless round of self-improvement did not spend it any other way; they lost it. Without a trace of humor More says that if a man has no aptitude for liberal sciences and "had rather bestow this time upon his own occupation . . . he is not letted nor prohibited."[8]

More did not impose compulsory bond labor on certain Utopians out of need for a work force to do the dirty jobs in the economy, as Kautsky suggests.[9] He did not need Utopians for compulsory labor because he set up three other reservoirs of labor to do the dirty work: Utopians who did it voluntarily out of a religious calling,[10] poor foreign laborers to whom bondage in Utopia seemed a lighter burden than freedom in their native lands and foreign criminals condemned to death in their homeland.[11] For vile tasks any one of these

[7] "feats, helping anything to the advantage and wealth of life"; *artium, quae faciant aliquid ad commodae vitae compendia,* L 218, E 82, C 97

[8] L 142-143, E 56, C 60-61

[9] Kautsky, p. 208.

[10] L 280-282, E 104-105, C 129-130

[11] L 221-222, E 83-84, C 99

sources of labor would have sufficed in the simple sense that if the author chose to declare it sufficient, the reader could hardly gainsay him. More is in fact quite specific on the function of bond labor imposed on Utopians; its economic effects are incidental; the purpose of the servitude is penal; Utopians are made bondsmen when they are bad Utopians.[12]

A society that imposes bond service on some of its own citizens for absenteeism[13] and contentiousness[14] among other things may be the best state of the commonwealth to More's mind; it is not a modern socialist's notion of the ideal society. Believing that all social ills are the consequences of the system of property, modern socialists are heavily committed to the faith that such ills will ultimately vanish as a consequence of the expropriation of the expropriators and the emergence of a classless society. But although More envisaged a great amelioration of evils in his ideal state, he did not envisage their disappearance—therefore the system of penal labor. And this might imply that More thought the roots of those evils went deeper than the social institutions amid which in his time or any other they flourished.

If compulsory labor was an integral element in the pattern of More's social thought, "the frugality of the Utopians," "the restriction of wants," was even more so. There is substantial agreement among modern economists, socialist and otherwise, that a market mechanism, or a reasonable facsimile of one, is the sole efficacious means for securing the optimum allocation of resources necessary for that optimum satisfaction of wants which is the ideal goal of both capitalist and socialist economic systems. Without the market mechanism and money to lubricate its operation, consumer preference cannot adequately be registered; allocation of resources becomes a half-blind guess; and the producer ends by producing

[12] L 222, E 83, C 99 [13] L 168, E 65, C 73 [14] L 272, E 102, C 126

what he or his boss wants produced, which does not necessarily correspond with what the consumer wants to consume. But the abolition of money and the virtual destruction of the market mechanism is fundamental to the Utopian society, as important perhaps as the community of property of which it is the complement.[15] So in Utopia the methods of allocating productive resources and distributing the final product tend to restrict the satisfaction of wants; from an economic point of view they are incredibly inept. The point is not that More was a bad economist and that he constructed a bad economic system. The point is that he was not an economist at all in fact or in aspiration, that he was not interested in constructing a technically sound economic system, and that the function of the socialist elements in the Utopian commonwealth is essentially non-economic just as More's attitude toward work and leisure is non-economic. Thus the easy demonstration that a market mechanism and money are essential to the optimum allocation of resources is determinative for modern socialists; they are thereby bound to accept markets and money on a socialist base because they are committed to the *economic* superiority of socialism, and the ultimate measure of that superiority is capacity to allocate resources for the satisfaction of wants. The same easy demonstration would leave More quite indifferent and his antipathy to a market economy and money quite intact. The Utopian economy does not justify itself as modern economies do by claiming to give men in the fullest measure the things they want; it is not based on the tacit assumption of modern economies that on the whole what men want is what they ought to have. The shadow of Bentham lies forward over Mill and Marx, Kautsky and Keynes—it does not fall backward over More. The justification for the Utopian system in all its aspects, economic and other, is that it provides all men with what they

[15] L 308, E 114, C 143

need in the measure that they need it; and while men ought to have what they need, they certainly do not need and ought not to have in full, or any other measure, whatever they happen to want. In *Utopia* there is no touch of the Benthamite doctrine that pushpin is as good as poetry, or better if more people want it. More not only limits the wants which the Good Society ought to satisfy; he also sets a ceiling on the quality and kinds of goods that properly may be produced to satisfy even those legitimate wants. What appear to be the economic institutions of Utopia—community of property, abolition of markets and money—are economic in form but not in purpose. Their strictly economic function is incidental. In More's eyes, as we shall see, they serve not economic but other and higher ends.

8. THE ROOTS OF UTOPIA AND ALL EVIL

We are better equipped to discover what those ends are now that we know that bond labor, abolition of markets and money, and restriction of wants by enforced community of consumption are of a piece with the abolition of private property and profit and with the obligation to toil—indispensable motifs in the total pattern of More's best state of the commonwealth. A society where wants are tightly bound up and where the penal power of the state is made daily conspicuous by men in heavy gold chains—this is no ideal society of Modern Socialism. Altogether missing from *Utopia* is that happy anarchist last chapter of modern socialism intended to justify all the struggle, all the suffering, all the constraint that we must undergo in order to reach it. *Utopia* does not end in an eschatological dream.

More simply did not believe that all the evil men do can be ascribed to the economic arrangements of society, and that those evils and the very potentiality for evil will vanish when the economic arrangements are rectified and set on a proper footing. More believed no such thing because in his view of men and their affairs there was a strong and ineradicable streak of pessimism. More's pessimism was ineradicable because it was part and parcel of his Christian faith. He knew surely, as a profoundly Christian man he had to know, that the roots of evil run far too deep in men to be destroyed by a mere rearrangement of the economic organization of society. His residue of pessimism leads More to provide even "the best state of the commonwealth" with an elaborate complement of laws drastically limiting the scope given to individual human desires and to arm its government with extensive and permanent powers of coercion. Although he was convinced that the institutions of the society that he knew provided the occasions for the evils he saw, he did not—and as a profoundly orthodox Christian he could not—believe that the evils were totally ascribable to the institutions. His probings led him to believe that the roots of the evils of sixteenth century Europe, though nourished in the rich black earth of an acquisitive society, were moistened by the inexhaustible stream of sin.

Underlying the whole catalogue of evils of his time he finds one or another of several sins. Luxury, gluttony, envy, vanity, vainglory, lust, hypocrisy, debauchery, sloth, bad faith and the rest all find an easy vent in the Christendom he knew, whose institutions seemed to him as if contrived to activate human wickedness and anesthetize human decency. Yet More does not give equal attention to all the kinds of sin; the realm of evil is not a republic of equals. The Deadly Sins themselves are not on an even footing in the Utopian Discourse. Gluttony and Anger get short shrift, Envy is there only as a counterfoil to a deadlier sin, and Lust, that whipping boy of our feeble latter-day Christianity, receives but a passing glance. The great triumvirate that rules the empire of evil, are Sloth, Greed, and Pride.

It is sloth that in More's day leads stout fellows able to work to enter into the idle bands of serving men; it is sloth that leads them to fill with drinking, gaming, and brawling the hours they ought to spend in honest toil.[1] It is sloth, the avoidance of labor, that the Utopians punish with bondage.[2] Yet although to More's mind idleness was among the most destructive cankers on the social body, although it preoccupied him as much as any other problem, he did not blame that idleness wholly on sloth. The lazy good-for-nothing scum that the great leave in their wake is conjured into being by the great men themselves, who provide their followers with the means of debauchery and vice. And it is not sloth but a greater sin that leads the great men to foster the infection of idleness in the body of the commonwealth.

Even above sloth in the hierarchy of sin lie greed and pride. In dealing with these two paramount sins More's Christian faith stood him in good stead. It provided him with a basic insight into the underlying pattern of evil, a pattern somewhat obscured by our modern climate of opinion. For he did not believe that greed and pride were on a parity with each other as sources of the social ills of his day, or that they offered equal obstacles to the establishment of the Good Society; but at this point it requires special care to read More's meaning right. The best known passage of *Utopia*, the attack on enclosure in the Dialogue section, is directed against the "inordinate and insatiable covetousness" of landlords and engrossers.[3] Much of the Discourse section, moreover, is taken up with variation after variation on a single theme: "The love of money is the root of all evil." Now the inordinate desire for riches is greed or avarice, and from this it would seem to

[1] L 45-51, 146; E 21-23, 57; C 13-15, 62
[2] L 168, E 65, C 73
[3] L 51-56, E 23-25, C 15-18

follow almost as a syllogism that greed was what More discovered as a result of his social analysis to be the fount and origin of the sickness of his own society. Yet it is not so. Greed was a sin, revolting enough in More's eyes; but it is not a sufficiently attractive vice to stand alone. Men are impelled to it not by its charms, but, like other animals, by fear of want. "*Why*," Hythloday asks, "*should anyone consider seeking superfluities, when he is certain that he will never lack anything? Indeed in all kinds of living things it is . . . fear of want that creates greed and rapacity*."[4] It is one of the perverse traits of the regime of private property, where each must make provision for and look after his own, that an amiable regard for his kin continually tempts man to the sin of avarice.[5]

But this sin, certain to beset a pecuniary society, is essentially a parasite on the insecurity inherent in that kind of society and has no roots of its own. It is sustained rather by the institutional roots of the property system itself. Even the rich, More suggests, realize this, and are "not ignorant how much better it were to lack no necessary thing than to abound with overmuch superfluity, to be rid out of innumerable cares and troubles, than to be *bound down*[6] by great riches."[7] If avarice were the great danger to society the Utopian commonwealth could be instituted along lines far less rigorous and repressive than those More prescribes. But avarice is not all. Fear of want makes for greed in all living creatures, including man; in man alone greed has a second set of roots

[4] "For why should it be thought that man would ask more than enough, which is sure never to lack? Certainly, in all kinds of living creatures, . . . fear of lack doth cause covetousness and ravine"; *Nam cur superuacua petiturus putetur is, qui certum habeat nihil sibi unquam defuturum? Nempe auidum ac rapacem . . . timor carendi facit, in omni animantum genere*, L 157, E 61, C 68

[5] L 300, E 111, C 139

[6] "be besieged with"; *obsideri*

[7] L 305, E 113, C 142

deeper in his nature even than fear. For men only of God's creatures are greedy out of "pride alone, which counts it a glorious thing to pass and excel others in the superfluous and vain ostentation of things."[8] Here, I think, lies the heart of the matter. Deep in the soul of the society of More's day, because it was deep in the soul of all men, was the monster Pride, distilling its terrible poison and dispatching it to all parts of the social body to corrupt, debilitate, and destroy them. Take but a single example: Why must the poor in Europe be "wearied from early in the morning to late in the evening with continual work like laboring and toiling beasts" leading a life "worse than the miserable and wretched condition of bondmen, which nevertheless is almost everywhere the life of workmen and artificers?"[9] Human beings are consigned to this outrageous slavery merely to support the enormous mass of the idle, and to perform the "vain and superfluous" work that serves "only for riotous superfluity and unhonest pleasure."[10] What feeds the unhonest pleasure that men derive from luxuries and vanities, or to use the phrase of a modern moralist, from conspicuous consumption and conspicuous waste? It is pride. Many men drudge out their lives making vain and needless things because other men "count themselves nobler for the smaller or finer thread of wool"[11] their garb is made of, because "they think the *value*[12] of their own persons is thereby greatly increased. And therefore the honor, which in a coarse gown they dare not have looked for, they require, as it were of duty, for their finer gowns' sake. And if they be passed by without reverence, they take it angrily and disdainfully."[13] The same sickness of soul shows itself in "pride in vain and unprofitable honors." "For what natural or true pleasure doest thou take of another

[8] L 157, E 61, C 68
[9] L 141, E 56, C 60
[10] L 146, E 57, C 62
[11] L 181, E 70, C 80
[12] "price"; *precii*
[13] L 195-196, E 75, C 87

man's bare head or bowed knees? Will this ease the pain of thy knees or remedy the frenzy of thy head? In this image of counterfeit pleasure they be of a marvelous madness *who flatter and applaud themselves with the notion of their own nobility.*"[14] It is to support this prideful and conceited "opinion of nobility" that men must be treated like beasts of burden to keep idlers in luxury. The great mass of wastrels bearing down on Christendom are maintained to minister to the pride and vainglory of the great. Such are "the flock of stout bragging rushbucklers,"[15] "the great . . . train of idle and loitering servingmen,"[16] that "rich men, especially all landed men, which commonly be called gentlemen and noblemen,"[17] themselves fainéants, "carry about with them at their tails."[18] Such too are the armies, maintained by those paragons of pride, the princes of Europe, out of the blood and sweat of their subjects, to sustain their schemes of megalomaniac self-glorification.[19] Thus seeking in outward, vain, and wicked things an earthly worship which neither their achievement nor their inner virtue warrants, Christians lure their fellow men into the sin of sloth, or subject them to endless labor, or destroy their substance, their bodies, and their souls too, in futile wars; and over the waste and the misery, over the physical ruin and the spiritual, broods the monster sin of pride.

The Utopian Discourse then is based on a diagnosis of the ills of sixteenth century Christendom; it ascribes those ills to sin, and primarily to pride, and it prescribes remedies for that last most disastrous infection of man's soul designed to inhibit if not to eradicate it. For our understanding of the Utopian Discourse it is of the utmost importance that we

[14] "which for the opinion of nobility rejoice much in their own conceit"; *ii qui nobilitatis opinione sibi blandiuntur ac plaudunt*
[15] L 146, E 57, C 62
[16] L 46, E 22, C 13
[17] L 146, E 57, C 62
[18] L 46, C 21-22, C 13
[19] L 81-87, E 35-37, C 31-34

recognize this to be its theme. Unless we recognize it, we cannot rescue More from the ideologically motivated scholars of the Left and the Right, both as anxious to capture him for their own as if he were a key constituency in a close Parliamentary election. According to the Rightist scholars, who have allowed their nostalgia for an imaginary medieval unity to impede their critical perceptions, More was one of the last medieval men. He was the staunch defender of Catholic solidarism represented in medieval order and liberties, in a stable, agrarian subsistence economy, in guild brotherhood, monastic brotherhood, and Christian brotherhood against the inchoate growth of modern universal otherhood, already embodied, or shortly to be embodied in nascent capitalism, the New Monarchy, Protestantism, and Machiavellianism.[20] On the other hand, the most recent exponent of the *Utopia* as an exemplification of dialectical materialism has seen More as a fine early example of the Middle Class Man whose social views are one and all colored by his antipathy to late medieval feudalism as represented in the enfeebled but still exploitative Church and in the predatory and decadent feudal aristocracy, making their final rally in the courts of equally predatory and decadent dynastic warrior princes.[21]

Both of these formulations—that of the Left and that of the Right—are subject to a number of weaknesses. They are both based on conceptions of economic development and social stratification in the sixteenth century and earlier more coherent than correct, and largely mythological in many respects. The Leftist scholars by regarding More's age from a particular twentieth century perspective, the Rightists by regarding it from what they fondly imagine to be a medieval

[20] Chambers, passim; Campbell, passim. I borrow the concept of modern "otherhood" from my friend Prof. Benjamin Nelson, *The Idea of Usury: From Tribal Brotherhood to Universal Otherhood*, The History of Ideas Series, 3.

[21] Ames, passim

perspective deprive both More's opinions and his age of the measure of internal cohesion that both in truth possess. But to document these criticisms adequately would require an inordinate amount of space.[22] For the moment it must suffice to point out that from *Utopia* and from the events of More's life, scholarly ideologues both of the Left and of the Right have been able to adduce a remarkable number of citations and facts to support their respective and totally irreconcilable views. Now this paradox is amenable to one of two possible explanations. The first would require us to assume that More's thought was so contradictory, disorderly, and illogical as to justify either of these interpretations or both, although in reason and common sense they are mutually contradictory. But the intellectual coherence and sureness of thought of the Utopian Discourse and the sense of clear purpose that it radiates seem to preclude this resolution of the paradox. The second possibility is that either point of view can be maintained only by an unconscious but unjustifiable underestimate of the weight of the citations and data offered in support of the opposite point of view, but that all the citations and data fall into a harmonious pattern if looked at in a third perspective.

The character of that third possible perspective I have tried to suggest: the Utopian Discourse is the production of a Christian humanist uniquely endowed with a statesman's eye and mind, a broad worldly experience, and a conscience of unusual sensitivity, who saw sin and especially the sin of pride as the cancer of the commonwealth. Now the social critic of any age is bound to direct his most vigorous attack at the centers of power in that age and reserve his sharpest

[22] I have touched on two aspects of the general problem of sixteenth century society in two recent articles, "The Education of the Aristocracy in the Renaissance," *Journal of Modern History*, 22, 1950, pp. 1-20; and "The Myth of the Middle Class in Tudor England," *Explorations in Entrepreneurial History*, 2, 1949-1950, pp. 128-140.

shafts for the men possessing it. For however great the potentialities for evil may be in all men, real present social ills, the social critic's stock in trade, are immediately the consequence of the acts and decisions of the men actually in a position to inflict their wills on the social body. In a pecuniary society enjoying a reasonable measure of internal security and order but subject to great disparities of wealth, the social critic is bound to attack the very rich, because in such a society, where direct violence does not bear all the sway, riches become a most important source of power. This does not necessarily imply that pride is wholly confined to rich and powerful men, although by their possession of and preoccupation with money and power, the two goods most highly prized by the worldly, they are sure to be especially vulnerable to that sin. It is more to the point, however, that the pride of the powerful is, by virtue of their power, socially efficacious, since it is armed with the puissance of command. It can get what it wickedly wants. In More's Europe—the illicit violence of lordship almost everywhere having been suppressed by the new monarchs—it was the pride of the rich that did the real wicked work in the world, the work of fraud, oppression, debauchery, waste, rapine, and death. So More's shafts find their target in the rich and the powerful—in the bourgeois usurer, the engrosser, the court minion, the mighty lord of lands and men, the princes of the earth, in the encloser and depopulator whether that encloser was a parvenu grazier-butcher still reeking of the blood of the City shambles or a predacious noble of immaculate lineage or an ancient abbey rich in estates and poor in things of the spirit. These were his target not because together they form a homogeneous social class, for they do not, nor because they are all decadently medieval or all inchoately modern, for they are not all one or all the other, but because their riches and power sustained the empire of pride over the world that More knew and whose social ills he had traced to that center of evils.

Once we recognize that More's analysis of sixteenth century society led him to the conclusion that pride was the source of the greater part of its ills, the pattern of the Utopian commonwealth becomes clear, consistent, and intelligible. In its fundamental structure it is a great social instrument for the subjugation of pride. The pecuniary economy must be destroyed because money is the prime instrument through the use of which men seek to satisfy their yet insatiable pride. It is to keep pride down that all Utopians must eat in common messes, wear a common uniform habit, receive a common education, and rotate their dwelling places. In a society where no man is permitted to own the superfluities that are the marks of invidious distinction, no man will covet them. Above all idleness, the great emblem of pride in the society of More's time, a sure mark to elevate the aristocrat above the vulgar, is utterly destroyed by the common obligation of common daily toil. It is through no accident, through no backwardness of the Tudor economy, that More makes the Utopian commonwealth a land austere and rigorous beyond most of the imaginary societies elaborated by his later imitators. Had he cared only to consider man's material welfare, his creature comfort, it need not have been so. More was a logical man; he knew that to bind up pride on all sides it takes a strait prison, and he did not flinch from the consequences of his diagnosis. As he truly says this "kind of vice among the Utopians can have no place."[23]

Since More does not explicitly speak of pride very often in *Utopia,* my emphasis on its role in his social thought on both the critical and constructive side may seem exaggerated. Let anyone who thinks this is so consider the words with which More draws Hythloday's peroration and the whole Discourse

[23] L 157, E 61, C 68

of the best state of a commonwealth to its conclusion: "I doubt not that the respect of every man's private commodity or else the authority of our Saviour Christ . . . would have brought all the world long ago into the laws of this weal public, if it were not that one only beast, the princess and mother of all mischief, Pride, doth withstand and let it. She measureth not wealth and prosperity by her own commodities but by the miseries and incommodities of others; she would not by her good will be made a goddess if there were no wretches left *over whom she might, like a scornful lady, rule and triumph,*[24] over whose miseries her felicity might shine, whose poverty she might vex, torment, and increase by gorgeously setting forth her riches. This hellhound creeps into men's hearts; and plucks them back from entering the right path of life, and is so deeply rooted in men's breasts that she cannot be plucked out."[25]

The disciplining of pride, then, is the foundation of the best state of the commonwealth. And more than that, it is pride itself that prevents actual realms from attaining to that best state.

9. THE UTOPIA OF A CHRISTIAN HUMANIST

So far we have found that More's Utopian Discourse rests on an acute appraisal of the ills of sixteenth century Christendom, and that its institutions are designed to destroy the roots of those ills. But this is rather negative and therefore not quite adequate. After all, the Utopian Discourse was also a work of construction; Utopia itself was something quite positive—the best state of the commonwealth. A study of the positive traits and ordering of that commonwealth should

[24] "whom she might be lady over to mock and scorn"; *quibus imperare atque insultare possit*

[25] L 305-306, E 113-114, C 142

give us some added insight into More's intention and beliefs, and also into his milieu, the milieu of the religious revival that preceded the Protestant Revolution. The conception of the community of property in *Utopia* has already proved so useful a base point for our investigations that we may do well to turn to it again to start our new exploration.

As has been pointed out the general conception of community of property and goods as a social desideratum of some sort or other was almost two thousand years old when More wrote *Utopia*. That at the time he wrote he was well acquainted with two ways of developing the conception, he indicates explicitly in the text of the work. We have already noticed that in connection with the community of property in Utopia he directly mentions Plato's *Republic*[1] and the rule of the monastic groups.[2] A third development of the idea of community of property, part of More's intellectual equipment when he wrote *Utopia*, though not mentioned there, is the idea of the community of all possessions as it appears in the writings of Seneca and the great Church Fathers. With the Stoic-Patristic idea, however, the conception of community of property in *Utopia*, and the function it performs there, have little in common. The idea as developed by Seneca and the Fathers never touched on practical matters; it had nothing to do with the problem of making the community of property work in any conceivable human society. This vagueness was a natural result of the role played by the community of property in their scheme of things. In that scheme community of property was in no sense exemplary; it was not a goal toward which existing societies might strive, however feebly, nor even an ideal against which they might be measured and their shortcomings noted. Community of property was not an institution of a society that might be or should be, but of a

[1] See above, Part One, section 3.
[2] See above, Part Two, section 4.

society that once was but could never be again. It belonged to the lost Golden Age, to the lost Eden, to an age of innocence which, once destroyed, can never be reconstituted this side of the grave. Once Pandora's box was opened, once the fruit of the Tree of the Knowledge of Good and Evil was tasted, the primitive communism of Seneca and the Fathers could be no more, and laws of property making clear the rules of thine and mine became necessary to keep mankind, fallen on evil days, from rending itself into bloody bits. Ultimately, then, the force of the Stoic-Patristic conception of community of property was to provide a justification for almost any legal system of property right, and at the same time by connecting them with man's fallen and imperfect state to deprive all property systems of sanctity or any high place in the hierarchy of human values.[3] Whatever the ultimate role of the community of property in the Utopian Discourse, it is not the Stoic-Patristic one. For that Discourse does not hark back to a universal Golden Age forever lost, and does not in any way justify the existence or deny the importance of the property arrangements of More's own day.

Plato's *Republic*, not only in its practice of community of property but in a number of other respects, is strikingly similar to *Utopia*.[4] There is the presence of abundant detail in both, and also the close correspondence of some of the particular details. In both Plato and More community of property is but part of a more general scheme of community of living and way of life, which includes both in the *Republic* and in *Utopia* prohibition of the use of money, common training in arms, community of habitation, education, and meals. All these things tend to enforce a rigid communal equality

[3] For a full exposition of Stoic and Patristic social theory, see R. W. and A. J. Carlyle, *A History of Mediaeval Political Theory in the West*, 6 vols., London, 1903-1936, I, pp. 1-194.

[4] Plato, *Republic*, passim

among the participants in the scheme, but beyond this common tendency More owes to Plato the very idea that the Utopian Discourse was built on. The *Republic* was the first and in many respects the greatest attempt to do what More attempted nearly two thousand years after—imaginatively to set forth an ideal model of the best state of the commonwealth. It is undeniably striking that More followed Plato in regarding community of property as indispensable to the ideal society. Less striking but hardly less significant are the ways that More, with the *Republic* in mind as he wrote, deviated from it in *Utopia*. Consider a single detail: the participants in Plato's scheme are emancipated from the daily round of common toil; to that daily round the Utopians with trifling exceptions are firmly bound. Plato's guardian minority lives off the labor of others; the Utopian community lives off its own labor. But in the light of this difference of detail the whole pattern of community of life as practiced in Utopia takes on a meaning quite at variance with the meaning of the same pattern in the *Republic*. The end of all regulations enforcing community of living in the *Republic* was invidious. It aimed at the isolation of an élite whose common way of life bound each to the other by the closest ties, and also separated the chosen few by a vast gulf from the subject herd, fit only to be ruled, who lived not as they. The immolation of the individual and of the human personality itself in the guardian group served to create a monolithic *esprit de corps* and group pride, and the relation of ruling guardians to ruled masses was not unlike the relation of Spartan to helot. So effectively and completely did community of living and *exemption from toil* in the *Republic* separate rulers from ruled that the code of truth, trust, and mutual confidence that applied among guardians was supplanted by a code of benign deception in their relations to the subjects. In Utopia, on the other hand, community of living and *obligation to toil* were the foundation of a society where the gap between rulers and ruled was made as narrow as the existence of effective authority allowed. They apply not to a *corps d'élite* but to all citizens; they were not aristocratic but egalitarian, not directed toward the creation and maintenance, but toward the annihilation, of invidious distinctions among men.

No more than the institutions of the *Republic* are the institutions of Utopia ends in themselves. They are part of the general conception of the best state of the commonwealth and, as we have seen, the obligation to toil and the community of living both serve toward that bridling of pride which to More is the indispensable foundation of the good society. And this brings us to the third formulation of the idea of community of property that More had in mind when he wrote the Utopian Discourse: the community of property and living commanded by the rules of the religious orders and practiced by the best religious houses. In detail the laws and ordinances of the Utopian commonwealth have about as much in common with the Benedictine Rule[5] as they have with the institutions of Plato's *Republic*. Besides the community of property and dwelling and the common meals, there are the strict regulations imposed on the movements of the individual when outside his prescribed precinct, the duty of common toil, the lecture at refection, the prescription of a uniform, simple, and unchanging habit, and the disciplinary force of the common surveillance of all one's doings; for as the monk has no privacy so the Utopian citizen was always "in present sight and under the eyes of every man."[6] The likeness between the monastic and the Utopian regimen is so striking and More's comparison of the latter with the former so explicit that the defense of the monastic way against the advance of secularism

[5] St. Benedict, *Regula Monasteriorum*, ed. C. Butler, Freiburg im Breisgau, 1935, passim.

[6] L 169, E 65, C 74

has been suggested by scholars to be one of the main themes of the Utopian Discourse.[7] And we have lately observed in that Discourse further support for those who find this suggestion persuasive, for we discovered that the underlying purpose of Utopian community of property and of the whole institutional framework of the Utopian commonwealth was the uprooting of pride.[8] But a similar purpose underlies the monastic discipline. Perfection in the monastic way was measured on an ascending scale at the bottom of which was the sin of pride, and progress in the religious life was in the main gauged by one's ascendancy over that sin. As among poverty, chastity, and obedience, St. Benedict's Rule while demanding all three gives most attention to obedience, especially the obedience of the monk to the abbot, because the self-surrender involved is the decisive step in the deracination of the pride of self-will.

Yet we ought not too readily accept the thesis that the Utopian Discourse is a defense of the monastic orders or that the Utopian commonwealth is merely an idealization of the monastic way of life and the Benedictine Rule. The first thesis is too subtle for the broad face values of *Utopia*, and implies paradoxically that More concealed his intention so successfully as to make *Utopia* a failure. For the notion that the Utopian Discourse was a defense of the monastic way seems to have occurred to none of More's contemporaries and to no one else up to a few years ago. A defense of the monastic way so refined as to escape notice for more than four hundred years despite the continuous popularity of the work in which it is embedded is a queer kind of defense. After all, the purpose of a polemic defense—as that practiced polemicist Thomas More well knew—is to give pause to assailants and force them back. But this purpose cannot be achieved by a defense so ethereal that the attacker does not know it is there. Erasmus, for example, in what he has to say about *Utopia* seems quite

[7] Chambers, p. 136

[8] See above, Part Two, section 8.

unaware that it is or involves a defense of the monastic way.[9] Yet in the summer of 1516 in England, when he first saw the Utopian Discourse, Erasmus must have been especially alert to anything like a defense of monastic life. Not only was he the most eminent living critic of the orders, he was in England at the very moment for the purpose of putting the final touches to an appeal for a papal dispensation that would relieve him of the dread that haunted him at the possibility of being called on to fulfill his own monastic vows.[10] Despite an exacerbated awareness of all that pertained to the monastic life, Erasmus saw no defense of monasticism in *Utopia*, although he did see several thrusts at the contemporary practices of the orders.[11] This is not to argue that More did not admire the monastic ideal or that he was unwilling to defend it. It is simply to argue that, however much he admired that ideal and however willing he was to defend it, he did not do so in *Utopia*.

It is his admiration for the monastic way that lends plausibility to the thesis that, without intending any specific defense of the orders, in *Utopia* More still found the monastic rule so attractive that he constructed his ideal commonwealth on the foundations it provided. This notion, supported by the evidence we have already drawn from the Utopian Discourse, gains further plausibility from what we know of the author. More hankered for the habit; all through his life an inclination, and something stronger than an inclination, to the cloister runs as a consistent and recurring theme. During four years of his legal studies at the Inns of Court he lived in the Charterhouse of London, where "he gave himself to devotion and prayer," sharing, as nearly as his work allowed him, in the way of living of the Carthusians.[12] So deeply did that

[9] L, marginal notes, passim [10] A 2:447, intro. [11] L 73-77, 287

[12] William Roper, *The Mirrour of Vertue in Worldly Greatness or the Life of Sir Thomas More, Knight*, London, 1903, p. 6.

way attract him that his ultimate decision not to follow it may well have been accompanied by a profound psychic crisis. His letter to Colet, written shortly before or shortly after the die was cast, is marked by an almost hysterical tension.[13] And a little later he chose to translate for a nun the biography of that learned, pious, and ambiguous Italian Giovanni Pico, who yearned for the monastic way, refused despite Savonarola's urging to take the vows of religion, and yet subjected himself to an ascetic discipline.[14] More's choice of a subject was probably not casual. He himself seems to have been seeking some way to combine the austerity of the cloister with a life in the world, and his quest was life-long. Besides leading his family in an extensive daily course of pious observances,[15] he built himself a place with a chapel and a library for prayer and study. On Fridays he used "continually to be there from morning till evening, spending his time only in devout prayers and spiritual exercises."[16] Even in his later years when he became Lord Chancellor of England he would say the church service in his private chapel in the surplice of a humble priest.[17] "Secretly next his body," his son-in-law Roper, who lived in his house for years, tells us, "he wore a shirt of hair. . . . He also sometimes used to punish his body with whips, the cords knotted."[18] At the end of his days More ascribed to his duty to his wife and children his failure to become a monk.[19] And as he saw three Carthusians cheerfully going the way to execution that he was soon to follow, he exclaimed to his daughter at the great difference God made "between

[13] Thomas More, *The Correspondence of Sir Thomas More*, ed. E. F. Rogers, Princeton, 1947, no. 3; Thomas Stapleton, *Life . . . of Sir Thomas More . . . (Part III of "Tres Thomae")*, tr. P. E. Hallett, London, 1928, pp. 11-13.

[14] Thomas More, "Life of John Picus, Earle of Mirandole," *The Works of Sir Thomas More, Knight*, ed. W. Rastell, London, 1557, pp. 1-34.

[15] Roper, p. 27 [16] *ibid.* [17] *ibid.*, pp. 50-51

[18] *ibid.*, p. 48 [19] *ibid.*, p. 74

such as have in effect spent all their days in a straight, hard, penitential, and painful life, religiously, and such as have in the world, like worldly wretches, as thy poor father hath done, consumed all their time in pleasure and ease licentiously."[20]

The life of religion loomed so large in More's imagination and there is so much of the monastic rule in *Utopia* that its presence cannot be passed off as casual. But here we must face the curious fact that so much of the monastic rule is *not* incorporated in Utopian institutions that its *absence* cannot be passed over as casual either. What is missing of the rule in Utopia is not merely regulations of celibacy nor a random scattering of other regulations; a whole segment of the cenobitic ethic is lacking. Like the Rules of the Religious the institutions of Utopia aim to level pride; unlike the Rules of the Religious they do not aim to inculcate humility, docility, and self-abasement. Yet More was far from denying that humility and self-abasement were virtues. Indeed he made special provision for their practice in the Utopian commonwealth itself. They were the way of life of those Utopians who thought that "felicity after this life was to be gotten by busy labor and good exercises. Some therefore of them attend upon the sick, some amend highways, cleanse ditches, repair bridges, dig turves, gravel and stones, fell and cleave wood, bring wood, corn and other things into the cities in carts, and serve . . . as servants, yea, more than bondmen. For whatsoever unpleasant, hard, and vile work is anywhere, from *which its wretchedness or their loathing deters others,*[21] all that they take upon them willingly and gladly, procuring rest and quiet to others, remaining in continual work and labor themselves. . . ."[22]

[20] *ibid.*, pp. 78-79

[21] "from the which labor, loathsomeness and desperation doth fraye other"; *a quo plerosque labor, fastidium, desperatio deterreat.*

[22] L 280-281, E 104-105, C 129-130

These men are divided into two sects, one of which "live single and chaste, abstaining not only from the company of women, but also from the eating of flesh. . . . Utterly rejecting the pleasures of this present life as hurtful, they be all wholly set upon the desire of the life to come, by watching and sweating hoping shortly to obtain it."[23] These men are revered and honored by the Utopians as most holy because "they say they be led to prefer single life before matrimony and that sharp life before an easier life . . . by religion."[24]

Here obviously we have the true Religious clearly marked off from the rest of the Utopians. There is special privation. There is the base labor to induce and foster a special humility. There is the special vocation, the religious calling. And finally there is the irrelevance of their existence to the social structure of the Utopian commonwealth. This "sect" is in nothing more like the monastic orders than in the independence of its internal structure from the society around it. Precisely because it is *not* of the world, it could exist anywhere in the world. But its very presence in Utopia serves to emphasize the difference between the best state of the commonwealth and a monastic community. Utopians do not subject themselves to extraordinary privation on religious grounds, their way of life is not organized to inculcate humility. Utopia is not a society which men enter voluntarily because of a special vocation, it is a society into which they are born; it is in short and despite all analogues a commonwealth, not a convent.

Indeed "there is in no place of the world, neither a more excellent people, neither a more flourishing commonwealth."[25] Yet we must once again return to the fact that "this fashion and form of a weal public" which More "would gladly wish unto all nations"[26] did employ methods similar to those of the Benedictine Rule to achieve a deracination of pride, which

[23] L 281, E 105, C 130
[24] L 282, E 105, C 130
[25] L 211, E 80, C 94
[26] L 306, E 114, C 142

was also one of the aims of that rule. The fruit of the destruction of pride in Utopia was not, however, as we have seen, a monkish humility. The result was not to reduce the proud to the posture of the meek and poor in spirit, since the Utopian citizen is never described as either meek or poor in spirit. Although the moral physiognomy of that citizen is never particularly set forth by More, the virtues imputed to him are not those that stand highest in the role of the ideal Religious—they are diligence, method, self-discipline, and self-respect. The polity of *Utopia* is after all a far cry from the despotic monarchy of the abbot over monks bound by a vow of unlimited obedience; it is rather an austere republic of self-respecting equals.[27] More, the man with a life-long hankering for the cloister, who yet gave himself to the life of the world, felt nevertheless that that life should draw closer to an ascetic ideal, that men without a special vocation could yet be a holy community by a life of labor and learning in a society of equals founded on a wise, just, and righteous law.

More's ideal was never realized of course; yet an attempt was made in sixteenth century Europe to impose on society something like a universal regimen of disciplined labor and learning to the greater glory of God. Because the institutional instruments were very different from those employed in Utopia and because the sponsor was a man of very different stamp from More, no line has ever been drawn connecting the later experiment with More's ideal. In this experiment the pride of the powerful was hewed down and the abjectness of the weak brought up to the level of self-respect not by the imposition of external badges of equality but by a reworking of the idea of the calling and by an amplification of the social meaning of the Sacrament of Communion. By attributing equal worth to all necessary vocations, and by imposing on all men the obligation to work in their earthly callings in the

[27] *Utopia,* Discourse, passim

same spirit of complete dedication and painful alertness to which the rule bound the Religious, the discipline of labor was laid upon all, while merit was imputed not to the earthly honor attached to the office, but to the zealous fulfillment of the tasks that the office required. By emphasizing the function of the Sacrament as a sign of participation in the community of saints and by guarding it from corruption by sinners through a rigorous surveillance of the private affairs of all citizens alike, the lines of social differentiation faded to insignificance in comparison with the line between those admitted to and those excluded from Communion. The need to protect the Sacrament from profanation made it possible and necessary to supervise the lives of all citizens, to destroy their privacy, and to subject all to a common rigorous discipline. It was the protection of the Sacrament that enabled the Consistory at Geneva to make their New Jerusalem into a place where, as in Utopia, all citizens were in effect "in the present sight and under the eyes of every man."

To suggest any significant relation between the Utopian dream of the gentle, smiling, kindly Catholic saint and the harsh reality that the grim Protestant hero Calvin reared at Geneva is sure to evoke protest; and unless the significance attached to the relation is carefully defined and circumscribed the protest will be justified. Actually, in suggesting such a relation we are only completing a triangle between three points, two of whose connecting lines have already been drawn by eminent scholars. The connection between Calvinism and the monastic ideal is firmly established in the work of Max Weber and Ernst Troeltsch.[28] The contrast lies between the *ausserweltliche Askese*—the asceticism of flight from the temporal order—of the monastery, that seeks perfection for the few in a rigorously regulated life in seclusion from the

[28] Max Weber, *The Protestant Ethic and the Spirit of Capitalism*, tr. T. Parsons, London, 1930, pp. 95-128; Troeltsch, 602-617.

world, and the *innerweltliche Askese*—asceticism within the temporal order—of Calvin that demands a striving toward such perfection from all men, who must continue to work in the world but who are to order their lives as if they were not of it. We have seen how scholars with Catholic prepossessions have assimilated the laws of the Utopian commonwealth to the ascetic rule of the "rightest Christian companies." But we have also noted the failure of these scholars to observe that More sets forth an ascetic way of life as an example and model not to specially called communities of Christian athletes, but to secular society at large, to the whole *Res Publica Christiana*.

This is not to suggest that More would have approved the doings at Geneva, which he probably would not have done. Nor is it to suggest that More influenced Calvin, for such influence would be of little importance in the pattern of Calvin's thought. Nor is it intended to imply that More was a proto-Calvinist, whatever that may be. But the point of spiritual contact between More and Calvin, above indicated, may make a curious and rather important aspect of sixteenth century history a little less perplexing. To most men today the creed of Calvin seems stern, forbidding, narrow, and repellent. For the favor of religiously-minded intellectuals of the present it has proved but a feeble competitor against Catholicism and Communism. Yet almost from the start and throughout the sixteenth century Calvinism seems to have exercised its most powerful attraction not on this or that economic class but on the intellectual élite of all classes. The force radiating from Geneva, bearing revolution through Western Europe, was not borne by armies with banners or traders with packs but by men who joined great learning with measureless zeal, whose chief weapon was words, or, as they would have said, the Word. Calvinism early drew to it ecclesiastics and monks; but laymen of broad learning and culture also felt its magnetism. The defense of the faith that Calvin built rallied to it the swords and pens and labors of men like du Plessy Mornay, Phillippe Marnix, and Francis Walsingham, men to whom Calvinist asceticism in this world had become a way of life. Nowhere in the sixteenth century did the strength of Calvinism rest on numbers. It was the quality of the men drawn to the creed that sustained the cause and with it the cause of Protestantism itself against the Catholic Counter-Reformation. It is at this point that the line we have drawn between More and Calvin may help our understanding. The Calvinist leaders were almost all in some measure products of the Christian humanist pedagogic tradition of which More was one of the founders. The kind of aspiration that drew these men toward Calvinism was not altogether alien to that tradition. It finds expression in More's own Utopian Discourse. It is the aspiration to remould human society into a holy community, to bring it into closer conformity to God's law by the imposition of a firm but just and righteous discipline on the daily life and doings of all citizens. In some measure Calvin created what More, but not More alone, yearned for—a more austere Christian life in a more rigorously Christian social polity. On foundations not at all Utopian he established that *innerweltliche Askese* of which the Utopian polity is itself an expression.

For several decades before the Reformation Europe had felt the stirring of a general religious revival. That revival in almost all its individual manifestations was marked by a distinctive trait; the various lines of access to the divine that men sought and believed they had found were relatively direct, relatively independent of that route of sacerdotal mediation, which by a divinely established monopoly the Catholic priesthood controlled. In this respect the revival, even when sponsored by churchmen like Erasmus, was a lay movement. Otherwise the revival was many-sided, complex, and ambivalent. It was the matrix of much that was to come in the succeeding two hundred years of the history of European thought and feeling—Platonism, Lutheranism, deism, rationalism, Catholic resurgence. The historians of these various movements have occasionally tended to stake out an exclusive claim to their common matrix, to insist that the revival was "essentially" Catholic, or "essentially" pre-Lutheran, or "essentially" rationalist. I am certainly not trying to prove that the revival was essentially Calvinist. It was rather a rich mulch of religious aspiration and unrest in which all these plants found sustenance. But a religious soil that can nourish both Trent and Geneva can hardly be claimed as the exclusive breeding ground of one or the other or of anything in between. And as to More, one of the greatest protagonists of the revival, we may doubt whether he would have found either Trent or Geneva much to his liking.

And so we finally reach our third point. In the Utopian Discourse, which he wrote in the Netherlands, More determines the nature and conditions of the Good Society. He bases his construction on a diagnosis of the maladies of the European polities of the early sixteenth century. His work throughout is marked by a concrete sense of detail, ability to grasp the interconnections of social phenomena, and shrewdness in devising remedies that attack the roots of social ills, as he conceived them. Yet if our analysis of the composition of the *Utopia* is correct, More was satisfied to close the book of his first intention—the Introduction and Discourse—without even the faintest suggestion of any means whereby European realms might be brought from their evil condition to the good state he envisaged. At first sight it seems most strange that one who so clearly saw the end should be so indifferent about the problem of the means necessary to attain it. To indicate why I do not believe that it was really strange at all, I will have to direct attention for a while away from the original version of *Utopia*—the Introduction and Discourse written in the Netherlands—to the Dialogue, the part More added *per occasionem* and *ex tempore* after his return to London.

Part Three: The Dialogue of Counsel

Part Three: The Dialogue of Counsel

1. *NUSQUAMA NOSTRA*

MORE, then, returned to England with the manuscript of a work at once remarkable and complete—the *Utopia* of his first intention. Naturally enough under the circumstances Peter Giles expected to see a polished version of this Discourse in a few weeks.[1] As we know, he saw nothing of the sort for almost a year,[2] and then what he did see was something more than the book he knew about. What More sent back to the Netherlands, in September 1516, was the original version of *Utopia*, plus a new ending, plus the brilliant Dialogue that he had inserted between the previously written Introduction and the Discourse of Hythloday[3] —a Dialogue that probed with great depth of feeling into a crucial problem of politics that the original Discourse by implication raised but did not deal with at all. Why did he add the Dialogue to *Utopia*? When and under what circumstances did he make the addition?

There is no positive data on which to base a sure answer to the last question; but a few significant events of the year between More's return to London from the Netherlands and his transmission of the final version of *Utopia* to Erasmus will allow us at least to make an educated guess. The first mention of *Utopia* in any surviving correspondence appears in the letter More sent to Erasmus along with the completed manuscript in September 1516. Its opening sentence is a little odd: "I send you our *Nowhere*, nowhere well written."[4] *Nusquamam nostram, nusquam bene scriptam ad te mitto. . . .* Now it was quite ordinary for a humanist "I" to talk about

[1] L I, E 7, C 250
[2] *ibid.*
[3] See above, Part One, section 4.
[4] N 2:381; A 2:461, line 1

"my work."[5] It was almost equally commonplace for a humanist to editorialize or regalize himself and talk about "we" doing "our work," but respect for reference seems to have inhibited writers from simultaneously designating themselves with a plural possessive (*nostram*) and a singular verb (*mitto*). So when More sends Erasmus "our *Utopia*," it suggests that the latter had a more active role in the creation of the book than is usually ascribed to him. But where and when did he play that role, and what part of *Utopia* did it affect? And what was the nature of that role? We may be sure that Erasmus did not himself write any part of *Utopia*. For that we have his own word in his letter to Hutten.[6] His word is fully supported by the fact that the only part of *Utopia* that he could have had any major influence on was the part he could not possibly have written: the Dialogue section with its intimate account of the household of Cardinal Morton, More's earliest mentor,[7] and its direct and oblique references to Royal policy under Henry VII[8] and to English economic life[9]—all probably beyond Erasmus' limited knowledge of English affairs. Of course Erasmus could have had nothing to do with the Introduction and Discourse which was the original version of *Utopia*. That part of the work, as we have seen, was done somewhere between the middle of May and the end of October 1515, in the Netherlands.[10] Now on his way from London to Basel late in May Erasmus almost certainly did see More in Bruges; but since Erasmus was still in London on May 21 and had already reached Mainz by June 1, the two friends could have had little time together on this occasion.[11] Besides, as his mission to the Netherlands was at that time barely two weeks old, More almost certainly

[5] e.g., Rogers, no. 31, lines 33-42
[6] N 3:398; A 4:999, lines 256-261
[7] L 40-78, E 20-34, C 10-29
[8] L 88-92, E 37-39, C 34-36
[9] L 45-58, E 21-26, C 13-19
[10] See above Part One, section 4.
[11] A 2:337 introductory notes, for Erasmus' movements at this date.

had not yet started writing *Utopia.*[12] Finally and decisively, More's natural courtesy would have prevented him from describing as "nowhere well written" a work in the composition of which his correspondent had had a hand.

The next meeting of the two old friends was not, like the meeting in Bruges, a few hours snatched in passing. Returning from Basel almost exactly twelve months after his journey thence, Erasmus spent over a month in and about Antwerp.[13] Part of this time he lived as a guest in Peter Giles' house,[14] and there he found waiting him a letter from More. In the letter the Englishman tells of his affection for Giles, and of his gratitude to Erasmus for opening up to him this new friendship, but he does not mention *Utopia.*[15] For what is was likely to add to the information already available to Erasmus on the subject, he had no need to mention it. Positive evidence could little enhance our certainty that when those two connoisseurs of letters, Erasmus and Giles, spoke of their absent friend, Giles told Erasmus of More's wonderful literary project so nearly complete when he last saw it almost a year ago, yet now vanished into a misty English silence. Surely Erasmus must have left the Netherlands for England with a reminder in his ears to find out what had become of that promising and promised book about the Island of Nowhere.

Arrived in London, Erasmus became a guest of the Mores, perhaps for about a month, long enough at any rate to feel by mid-August that he might be wearing thin his welcome not with his infinitely hospitable host Thomas, but with his slightly shrewish and parsimonious hostess Alice.[16] We may be sure that while he lived with the Mores Erasmus read, pondered, and discussed with its author the lively book Giles

[12] Rogers, no. 11, lines 9-13

[13] A 2:410-441

[14] N 2:261. The mention of Giles as Erasmus' host seems to confirm Nicholls' dating of this letter as against Allen's. A 2:388, intro.

[15] N 2:256-62; A 2:388

[16] N 2:320; A 2:451, lines 19-20

had told him about. We may be sure, too, that during the midsummer evenings the two old cronies, irrepressible lovers of good conversation, talked of many other things—of their own affairs, and prospects, of how the world had wagged in the year since they had last seen each other, perhaps of how it might be made to wag a little better. Less than three weeks after Erasmus left More's house his friend sent him *Utopia* with the Dialogue added—the final version ready for publication.[17] This sequence of events suggests as much about the circumstances surrounding the writing of the Dialogue section of *Utopia* as More's letter to Giles did about the writing of the Discourse section. We can now offer a reasonable conjecture why *Utopia*, beyond a doubt wholly written by More, could yet be the *Nusquama nostra* of More and Erasmus. We can also guess why Erasmus was so certain that the Dialogue section was written, *per occasionem* and *ex tempore*.[18] He was so certain because the special occasion of the addition of the Dialogue was, in a general way, Erasmus' visit with More and some of the things they talked about in a summer month. He knew it was composed *ex tempore* because he was on the premises where and when it was being extemporized, knocked off by More amid the press of business. And More a month later felt impelled to indicate Erasmus' share in the work with his *Nusquama nostra* because the part he wrote last had as its theme a subject they had carefully explored during Erasmus' visit. For reasons that we shall shortly explain it was perhaps the subject that they talked about most. The subject was counsel, and the main section of what More added to the *Utopia* in 1516 is a Dialogue of Counsel.

[17] N 2:381; A 2:461, line 1
[18] N 3:398; A 4:999, lines 259-60

2. THE CALL TO COUNSEL: MORE'S PERSONAL PROBLEM

Problems concerning the counseling and advising of princes had been a matter of increased personal interest to both Erasmus and More since they last saw each other at Bruges. Only a day or two after that meeting, on his way through Malines to Basel, Eramus first had broached to him the suggestion that he become the councilor of a prince—Archduke Charles of Burgundy, ruler of his homeland, emperor-to-be.[1] The job, of course, was to be a sinecure.[2] Apparently the sole permanent stipulation was that Erasmus should make the Netherlands his more or less permanent residence.[3] As a further condition Erasmus seems to have been required to sing one song for a promised lifetime of suppers. The song duly produced was the *Education of a Christian Prince*, which is at least as close to *bel canto* as it is to politics—a work whose literary flair alone distinguishes it from the wretched and dreary norm of the species, *De Regimine Principum*, of which it is a member. Still despite the duties of his post and the merits of his book—both about nil—when Erasmus saw More in London he was both a royal councilor and the author of a formal treatise of advice to princes, neither of which had he been a year before when he saw his friend in Bruges.

The concurrent developments of More's own career were marked by no such official or literary evidence of change, yet they were both more complex and more fateful. Up to the time of his mission to the Netherlands More had made his career entirely outside the orbit of royal favor and patronage despite his father's eminence in the legal profession, his own business contacts with the highest officials, and his extensive acquaintance among the inner circle of royal servants. His

[1] A 2:370, lines 16-23 and note. [2] *ibid.*
[3] *ibid.*

official services to the commonwealth up to 1515 were limited to those unpaid labors on commissions of the peace, sewers, and so forth, that English sovereigns time out of mind had exacted from their more substantial subjects as the price of their prominence and for the privilege of being Englishmen.[4] The Netherlands mission set More on the path of court service. Despite some early balking he followed that path to the end, which he found at the scaffold two decades later. Still, when he came back to England from the Netherlands late in 1515, the die, to his mind, was not cast. For the first time, however, a vigorous effort was being made to draw More into the King's service.[5] And thus also for the first time he was forced to think through the pros and cons of a career as councilor and courtier not only in relation to his immediate needs, wishes, and tastes, but in relation to his conception of the duty of a Christian man and a loyal subject of Henry VIII.

Immediate and personal needs loomed large for the returning envoy in that early sixteenth century winter. When More got back to England he seems to have been temporarily in narrow financial straits. A man who required little for himself but a great deal to support his liberality to others, More conformed to the Biblical injunction against hoarding for the morrow with an effortless ease that drove his thrifty second wife to distraction. He probably had little to spare when he left England for Bruges, and the longer he remained abroad the more embarrassed his finances were bound to grow. His regular income from the fees of litigation ceased, and his stipend from the King was about half of what he could have earned easily in London.[6] For six months in the Low Countries he had to maintain the state appropriate to the ambassador of a high

[4] See Appendix A.

[5] N 2:260; A 2:388, lines 127-136

[6] More seems to have been paid about £120 for his half year of service in the Netherlands (Ames, pp. 189-190). Roper says that in his legal work in London, More "gained without grief not so little as £400 by the year" (Roper, pp. 8-9).

and mighty king, and as he wrily observed, though "a kind father, . . . an indulgent husband, and . . . a considerate master . . . I have never been able to induce my family to go without food during my absence."[7] In short, his mission to the Netherlands involved him for half a year in twice his ordinary expense at about half his ordinary income. Little wonder that, writing to Wolsey when the mission was only in its second month, Tunstall had to include a special plea for "Master More" who, "at this time, as being at low ebb, desires by Your Grace to be set on float again."[8]

The financial dreariness of his immediate present may have brought sharply to More's mind the prospect of a yet drearier future. In the decade to come his pecuniary responsibilities were sure to reach peak load. He had his wife to support, and he had three daughters just approaching their teens. They all must be educated on the rather lavish scale that More's generous standards for female schooling required; and when that was done, before the decade was out, he would probably have to find dowries for them all. Then there was son John, seven years old at the time, also to be educated and started in his career. More had just incurred or was just about to incur another expense in the marriage of his step-daughter Alice Middleton;[9] and his foster daughter Margaret Giggs whom he loved and nurtured as one of his own had to be provided for, too.[10]

Under the circumstances it is hardly surprising that after his mission to Flanders More wrote with a touch of envy and even of malice about the cozy position of ambassadors in

[7] N 2:260; A 2:388, lines 121-124

[8] *Letters and Papers of the Reign of Henry VIII*, 2, no. 679.

[9] E. M. G. Routh, *Sir Thomas More and His Friends*, Oxford, 1934, p. 46 n. 2; Nicholas Harpsfield, *Life and Death of Sir Thomas More . . .*, ed. E. V. Hitchcock with historical notes by R. W. Chambers, Early English Text Society Publications, original series, 186, pp. 312-313.

[10] Routh, pp. 46-47, 131, 143

holy orders who "either have no wives and children or find them wherever they go" and whom "it is easy for princes to compensate for their labors with church preferments without putting themselves to any cost, while we laymen are not provided for so handsomely or so readily."[11] Nor is it surprising that in a passage of *Utopia* written in the Netherlands, More's own predicament bore fruit in an outburst, possessed of a particular and private poignancy, on the happy economic arrangements of the blessed Islanders who could "*be secure about the livelihood and happiness of their wives, children, grandchildren and their posterity.*"[12] To More, strapped for cash, with four children of the flesh, a stepchild and a foster child to look out for and with Dame Alice to wife, the prospect of living "*joyfully and tranquilly without any worry,*"[13] must have appeared as alluring as it was remote and improbable—a Utopian prospect indeed.

So Thomas More came back to London in the late autumn of 1515 with a successful mission to his credit and with a painfully collapsed purse. He came back to face the alternative of resuming his legal business or of entering the royal service on a permanent footing. The latter alternative was offered him by the two men in England most accustomed to having their own way and least inclined to take no for an answer: Thomas Wolsey and Henry Tudor. While More was in the Netherlands Wolsey, already Archbishop of York, had received his Cardinal's hat, and on Christmas Eve, 1515, he became Lord Chancellor in place of Archbishop Warham.[14] It was through Wolsey—perhaps at his instigation—that Henry sought to bring More to court. For once these two masterful men were balked of their desire a while. After receiving the overture

[11] N 2:260, A 2:388, lines 124-127

[12] L 300, E III, C 139. For translation, see above Part Two, section 5, note 17.

[13] *ibid.*

[14] A. F. Pollard, *Wolsey*, London, 1929, pp. 55-58.

More wrote Erasmus, "On my own return I had a yearly pension offered me by the King, which whether one looked to the honor or the profit of it was not to be despised. This, however, I have hitherto refused, and shall, I think, continue to do so, because, if I took it, the place I now hold in the City, which I prefer to a higher office, would either have to be given up, or retained—much to my regret—with some offense to the citizens, who, if they had any question with the government, as sometimes happens, about their privileges, would have less confidence in me, as a paid pensioner of the King."[15] It was surely his office as Under Sheriff of London rather than his legal practice that More felt so reluctant to give up. To the extent that London could lay claim to an urban patriciate of the continental type—and that was a very limited extent[16]—More was a part of it[17] and he had a bias in favor of the semi-independent quasi-republican polity that great European towns enjoyed by virtue of their charters of privilege—a bias that shows itself in the constitution of the Utopian commonwealth. The Under Sheriff was in effect the judge in the Sheriff's Court; but although More seems to have enjoyed his judicial work, it could hardly have been here that he rendered that service to the citizens in relation to the royal government that he was unwilling to jeopardize by accepting a pension from the King. But the Under Sheriff also seems to have done part of the work of representing the City in the law courts as a sort of assistant corporation counsel under the Recorder, the City's chief law officer. To the Recorder, the most important of the City's permanent appointed officials, the Under Sheriff had some prospect of

[15] N 2:260; A 2:388, lines 127-136

[16] Sylvia Thrupp, *The Merchant Class of Medieval London*, Chicago, 1948, pp. 191-233; *The Prologues and Epilogues of William Caxton*, ed. W. J. B. Crotch, Early English Text Society, original series, 176, pp. 77-78.

[17] Ames, p. 42.

succession.[18] It was probably this work, and perhaps this prospect, that More was unwilling to surrender for a royal pension in 1516.[19] But he hardly could have made a living as Under Sheriff even if he had acted parsimoniously, much less when he behaved in that habitually open-handed manner which Erasmus describes: "The office which is by no means burdensome, inasmuch as the court sits only on Thursdays before dinner, is considered highly honorable. . . . In most cases More remitted the fees which are due from the litigants, the practice being for the plaintiff to deposit three groats before the hearing, and the defendant a like sum, and no more being allowed to be exacted."[20]

Since he could not possibly have supported his household from the fees of his office, it must have been on his private legal practice that More depended for the larger part of his income. Given the choice between serving the City and serving the Crown, he might have chosen the City. But the alternative of court service or private legal practice was another story. More loathed litigation. He had been dragooned into the legal profession by his father,[21] and few men have even been so successful in a calling they liked so little. His revulsion against the practice of law shows through in the *Utopia* not only in repeated sardonic thrusts at the lawyers,[22] but in his startling characterization of the legal system itself as a device used by the dominant economic classes to keep the oppressed classes under heel. "The rich men not only by private fraud but also by common laws do every day pluck and snatch away from the poor some part of their daily living. . . . Now they have to this their wrong and unjust dealing . . . given the name

[18] N 3:395-396; A 4:999, lines 205-213; see Appendix B.
[19] Routh, p. 92, a. 3; Harpsfield, pp. 312-313
[20] N 3:395-396; A 4:999, lines 206-212
[21] N 3:393, A 4:999, lines 142-146
[22] L 43-47, 71, 234-236; E 20-22, 31, 88-89; C 11-14, 26, 105-106

of justice, yea and that by force of a law." The rich work out means to keep all they have entirely secure and "to hire and abuse the work and labor of the poor for as little money as may be. *Where the rich once in the name of the public including the poor have decreed that they shall be observed, these machinations are made into law.*"[23]

More's distaste for legal work seems to have mounted throughout the year after his return from the Netherlands. In a letter to Erasmus written in June he complains that he is losing all the learning he ever had, and explains that this is bound to be the case "with one constantly engaged in legal disputation so remote from every kind of learning."[24] In December he writes that he had a dream of being king in Utopia, but "the break of day dispersed the vision, desposing poor me from my sovereignty, and recalling me to prison, that is, to my legal work."[25] This mounting revulsion is particularly significant in 1516 when More was so clearly at the crossroads of his career. One sign pointed to the court, the other to a life filled with hateful legal business. He detested law business and the road to court was still wide open to him. Yet although the King and the King's chief minister were urging him on, More held back for fully two years before he made his final commitment. At no time during those two years could the unsettled crisis of his career have been far from the forefront of his mind.

So when Erasmus came to London More had successfully repelled the first advances of the prince, but he was still frequently in the presence of the King's all powerful minister, and he knew that a high place in the royal service was his for

[23] "These devices when the rich men have decreed to be kept and observed for the commonwealth's sake, that is to say, for the wealth also of the poor people, then they be made laws"; *ubi semel diuites publico nomine, hoc est etiam pauperum, decreuerunt obseruari, iam leges fiunt,* L 302-304, E 112, C 140-141

[24] N 2:293; A 2:424, lines 6-12

[25] N 2:443; A 2:499, lines 39-61

the taking.[26] If my guess is correct he argued the question "to take or not to take" with his old friend; and the distilled essence of the conversations that the problem evoked found its way as the Dialogue of Counsel into the final version of *Utopia*. Such at least seems to me the most plausible explanation of the presence of that section in the book.

3. THE CALL TO COUNSEL: THE STATESMAN'S PROBLEM

During the latter half of the fifteenth century and the first quarter of the sixteenth two problems had stood at the forefront of thought about politics—the problem of securing good governance for commonwealths and that of securing sound counsel for princes. Men who gave much thought to those problems recognized that in Europe at the turn of the century the solution of the first problem was contingent on the solution of the second. They would have concurred with More's judgment that "from the prince as from a perpetual wellspring comes among the people the flood of all that is good or evil."[1] And so they agreed that the peoples of Europe could fare well and be rightly governed only if their princes received the best advice of the best councilors, and having received it, accepted it.

The humanist writers of prince books seem to have treated the question of counsel with bland banality, skipping all the hard parts of the problem. In his remarks on counsel in the *Education of a Christian Prince*, written shortly before his visit to London in 1516, Erasmus exhibited the deficiencies of this species of humanist exercise. He says that the prince

[26] N 2:243; A 2:389, lines 62-64

[1] L 37, E 19, C 9; Seyssel, folio 16verso, ". . . en cestuy estat monarchique le tout depend de monarque. . . ."

ought to be uncorrupt and see to it that his whole household is uncorrupt, since the hatred aroused by his followers' vices falls on him. He feels that this part of a prince's task is easy, since it can be accomplished by summoning only good men to the royal service.[2] He further states that councilors should be sagacious and trustworthy;[3] and this is about the sum of the advice that Erasmus has to offer princes on one of the most pressing practical questions that they had to cope with.

The statesmen writers already referred to also busied themselves with the problem of counsel; but since they were incapable of the type of high-sounding nonsense the humanists indulged in, their investigations of the subject form tiny separate oases of political intelligence in a circumambient intellectual barrens. The most notable efforts were those of the English judge, Fortescue; the councilor of Louis XII, Claude Seyssel; and the diplomat Commynes. None of them was satisfied merely to inflate with lovely words and decorate with classical tags the hoary cliché about virtuous rulers choosing virtuous advisers. In the *Governance of England* Fortescue performed a remarkably subtle analysis of the structure of English polity, demonstrating the complex interdependence of fiscal reform, improvement of the administrative service, and the staffing of the king's council with reliable advisers.[4] A fourth of Seyssel's study of the administration of the French monarchy is given over to the problem of the internal structure and management of royal councils.[5] He calmly faces up to the fact that power pressures from without and power tensions from within the conciliar structure prevent it from ever being the totally disinterested symposium of virtuous men of the humanist dream, and he tries to elaborate an institutional

[2] Desiderius Erasmus, *The Education of a Christian Prince*, tr. and ed. L. K. Born, New York, 1936, p. 211.

[3] *ibid.*, pp. 194-195

[4] Fortescue, pp. 116-157

[5] Seyssel, folios 18verso-24recto

mechanism that will make sound advice available to the prince despite the power problems that the concentration of authority inevitably generates.[6] On one view of Commynes' *Mémoires* they are a continuous painstaking documentation of the thesis that the capacity for getting and taking sound advice is the key to the power of princes. The triumph of his protagonist Louis XI is a triumph of good counsel achieved against incredible odds by a ruler who spared neither time, nor effort, nor expense to get for himself and away from his enemies the ablest advisers the times afforded and money could buy. At the other extreme stood Louis' antagonist, Charles the Rash, whose catastrophic fall and dreary death were not merely the measure of Louis' skill in getting good advice but also of Charles' failure to keep good councilors, such as Commynes himself, in his service, to get sound advice, or to take it on the rare occasions when it was offered him.[7]

More's treatment of this paramount problem of counsel is uniquely determined by his unique position. In his intellectual affinities—his sense of concrete political process, his acute perception of political exigencies, and his skill at penetrating beneath the surface to the roots of political troubles—More belongs with the statesmen writers. But if his head belongs to them his heart belongs to the Christian humanists. This peculiar combination of heart and head linked with More's unusual moral sensitivity resulted in a kind of political perception unique in his own time and rare at any time. When More seriously focused that unique perception on the question of counsel the insight he achieved was sure to be something fresh and new.

[6] *ibid.*, esp. folios 23recto-24recto [7] Commynes, passim

4. THE CALL TO COUNSEL: A CHRISTIAN HUMANIST DILEMMA

It was, as we have seen, the King's offer and the difficulties of his own personal situation that first forced More to consider the problem of counsel. No doubt a man like Wolsey at once called to More's attention the honor and the profit that came to its recipient from a royal pension.[1] Yet however effective such considerations might be in focusing his attention, they could never determine More's decision. On the very first page of the Dialogue of Counsel, in what may be a recapitulation of his own thought processes, More sets forth the persuasions of profit, honor, and power as grounds for entering a prince's service only to set them aside once and for all. Like Hythloday More was "desirous neither of riches nor of power,"[2] or at least not sufficiently desirous to permit the most fateful decision of his life to be made on so self-regarding a basis. On the other hand his intensely personal predicament in 1516 did not suggest to him that cool analytical treatment of the problem of counsel from the ruler's point of view that characterized the investigations of the statesmen writers. So setting aside the private crisis that turned his attention to the question and slighting the exigencies and requirements of the rulers of the earth, More treats the problem of counsel wholly from the standpoint of the potential councilor. He seeks to determine the extent, if any, of a man's obligation to enter the service of a prince who seeks his aid in ruling the commonwealth.

More uses as a starting point for his Dialogue on Counsel a humanist dilemma of which Erasmus, its most persistent exemplar, was apparently unconscious. The dilemma goes

[1] See above Part Three, section 2.

[2] L 36-37, E 18, C 8. The argument from profit and honor is given to Peter Giles in the Dialogue.

something like this: as one of his first duties a king must seek good, wise, and learned councilors to keep him in the path of virtue. But the courts of kings are nests of evil, ruled by flattering sycophants and vicious gilded hypocrites. From such a milieu no good things can be hoped for; it taints and corrupts the best of men, diverts them from learning, involves them in shady practice, and deteriorates them in body, mind, and spirit. Good, wise, and learned men will flee such a certain source of pollution. Now if good, wise, and learned men followed Erasmus' precept and example it is hard to see how princes could follow his teaching; and it is perhaps the best evidence of the superficiality of the humanist social criticism of which he was the leading protagonist that Erasmus never felt impelled to reconcile these patently contradictory positions either in his writings or in his mode of life. More, however, was not the man to avert his eyes from a moral paradox or double back and take the expedient way around it. He was a moral athlete and when he found himself faced with an ethical dilemma he had to wrestle with it. It was precisely his unwillingness to take the easy way around such a dilemma that twenty years later was to lead to his martyrdom. So in 1516, with his career rather than his life at stake, he had to wrestle with the implications of court service for a Christian humanist. If in the Discourse section of *Utopia* Hythloday expresses More's opinions, in the Dialogue section he represents More's person. Hythloday is a Christian humanist to whom the opportunity to serve in the councils of a Christian prince is presumably available. Knowing what the courts of sixteenth century Christian rulers are like, his ideals and capacities being what they are, is he or is he not bound to render service to a prince? This is Hythloday's problem; it is also More's problem in 1516, since his ideals, capacities, and opportunity coincide precisely with Hythloday's.

More was a Christian humanist; therefore he was an intellectual—a man who in one of his social roles was devoted to cultivating and formulating knowledge. As a Christian humanist he was also an alienated intellectual—an intellectual who did not accept the validity of the assumptions, objectives, and rewards of the power system of the culture he lived in. Finally as a Christian humanist and, because of the precise and coherent character of his opinions, above all other Christian humanists, he was actively concerned to further social innovation. And now the government whose policy would have to be the vehicle of any major peaceful social innovation had invited him into its bureaucracy.[3]

The decision that an opportunity to enter the service of a great prince imposed on Christian humanists was difficult and intricate. These men, as we have seen, believed they had a comprehensive vocation to remake the world they lived in—to revive learning, to restore ethics, to rectify the social order, and to reform the Church. In the fufillment of their mission, what was to be gained by accepting court service, and what lost? And what would be gained and what lost by avoiding court service? The Dialogue of Counsel answers explicitly the first pair of questions; but in that Dialogue only once or twice does More give us a fitful flash of insight into the positive and powerful attraction that the life of the unattached intellectual held for the reforming humanist, not as a haven of withdrawal but as a sure base for the good fight. That attraction was connected with the pedagogic ideals of the Christian humanists, and we can begin to assess its significance by turning back to the Utopian Discourse, written, let us remember, when More himself was an intellectual still secure in his unattachment.

[3] The general formulation employed to describe More's position draws its terminology from Robert K. Merton, "Role of the Intellectual in a Public Bureaucracy," *Social Forces*, 23, 1945, pp. 405-415.

5. THE EDUCATION OF CHRISTENDOM

We have seen how important a role what More called good laws and ordinances, and what we should call sound political, economic, and social institutions, played in the Utopian commonwealth. We have as yet said almost nothing of the role of education in the Good Society. As all Utopians toiled, so all received schooling, boys and girls alike.[1] Their education did not stop when manhood and man's work began. On the contrary, the entire commonwealth daily transformed itself into an elaborate sort of extension program open to all citizens.[2] Although the schedule of study is not altogether clear, lectures seem to have begun a little after four in the morning and to have ended a little before nine when the period of daily labor began.[3] Despite the inordinately early hour, most Utopians flocked to these lectures. Nor is the cultivation of the mind in Utopia confined to this sunrise session. Self-improvement goes on all through the day. "They begin every dinner and supper by reading something that pertains to good manners and virtue"; and even during mealtime the elders subject the young to what sounds suspiciously like a politely conducted oral examination.[4] In the time between supper and bed at eight they engage in music or in educational and didactic games including a sort of allegorical chess, "in which game is very properly showed both the strife and discord that vices have among themselves, and again their unity and concord against virtues," and so on *ad infinitum* and *nauseam*.[5] Although More tries not to attribute to the Utopians any exceptional trait of character to raise them above the common run of men, he does, perhaps unconsciously, endow them with an incredible appetite for learning. As he says, though not overly fond of physical labor the Utopians "in the exercise

[1] L 183, E 71, C 81 [2] L 143, E 56, C 60-61 [3] *ibid.*
[4] L 165-166, E 64, C 71-72 [5] L 144-145, E 56-57, C 61

and study of the mind . . . be never weary."[6] The Utopians receive technical instruction in agriculture and a trade or two,[7] and also study the humanities and the sciences,[8] but the ultimate aim of education is neither technical nor cultural. Teachers are "not more diligent to instruct children in learning than in virtue and good conduct. For they use very great endeavor and diligence to put into the heads of their children while they be yet tender and pliant, good opinions and profitable for the conservation of their weal public. Which when they be once rooted in children, do remain with them all their life after, and be wondrous profitable for the defense and maintenance of the state of the commonwealth, which never decayeth but through vices rising of evil opinions."[9]

Such is the exalted conception More holds of the function of education in the best state of the commonwealth. Along with sound laws and institutions it creates the kind of citizen indispensable for the survival of that state. "The wholesome and virtuous opinions, wherein they were brought up even from their childhood, partly through learning, and partly through the good ordinances and laws of their weal public augment and increase their manful courage."[10] They are able to get along with few laws because "for . . . people *so well educated*[11] very few do suffice."[12] And punishment falls with a heavy hand on erring Utopians, "because they being so goodly brought up to virtue in so excellent a commonwealth, could not, for all that, be refrained from misdoing."[13] Indeed their whole ethos, and particularly that part which eradicates pride from their spirit, they attain to "partly by education, being

[6] L 212, E 81, C 95
[7] L 139-140, E 55, C 59-60
[8] L 143, 184; E 56, 71; C 61, 82
[9] L 284-285, E 106, C 132
[10] L 258, E 97, C 118
[11] "so instructed and instituted"; *sic institutis*
[12] L 234, E 88, C 105
[13] L 222, E 83, C 99

brought up in that commonwealth whose laws and customs be far different from these kinds of folly, and partly by good literature and learning."[14] And thus instruction and institutions together are the pillars of the best state of the commonwealth; together they are also the education of the Utopians.

We have already observed two of the main preoccupations of More's life reflected in *Utopia*: social reconstruction through sound *police* and the extension of an ascetic discipline in men's daily lives. Here we have the reflection of another of those preoccupations: reform of life and society through education. The same profound concern with education, the same estimate of its importance that he ascribes to the Utopians, More himself displays in many ways, but in none so vigorously and persistently as in his intense interest in the education of his own children. Affairs of state were to absorb his time and draw him away from many other affairs, but he never allowed them to overlay his zeal for the proper rearing of his brood.[15] Writing his children, he addresses the letter "To His Whole School" because "no one is dearer to me by any title than each of you by that of scholar. Your zeal for knowledge binds me to you almost more closely than the ties of blood."[16] Justly Erasmus describes his friend's household as "a school for the knowledge and practice of the Christian faith."[17] The most intimate revelation of More's views on the ends and uses of education occurs in a letter of advice and instruction to William Gonnell, the tutor of his children.[18] He first rejects the belief that mere learnedness is necessarily meritorious. "Though I prefer learning joined with virtue to

[14] L 183, E 71, C 81

[15] Rogers, nos. 43, 69, 107; Stapleton, pp. 106-111

[16] Rogers, no. 101, lines 4-7; Stapleton, p. 105

[17] Stapleton, p. 94

[18] Rogers, no. 63; Stapleton, pp. 101-104. Subsequent quotations concerning More's attitude on education are all drawn from this very important letter.

all the treasures of kings, yet renown for learning when it is not united with a good life is nothing else than splendid and notorious infamy." Yet learning should and may be a great aid to virtue by placing human concerns in their proper perspective.

"A soul must be without peace which is ever fluctuating between elation and disappointment from the opinions of men. Among the benefits that learning bestows on men there is none more excellent than this, that by the study of books we are taught in that very study to seek not praise but utility. . . . He . . . raises the character, who rises to virtue and true goods, and who looks down with contempt from the contemplation of what is sublime on those shadows of good things which almost all mortals through ignorance of truth greedily snatch at as if they were true goods." More seeks to have his wife, his friends, and his children's tutor join him in teaching his brood to avoid pride and set a low value on riches and vain display; "to put virtue in the first place, learning in the second; and in their studies to esteem most whatever may teach them piety towards God, charity to all, and Christian humility in themselves. . . . These I would consider the genuine fruits of learning, and though I admit that all literary men do not possess them, I would maintain that those who give themselves to study with such views, will easily attain their end. . . ."

As More goes on with his letter he unconsciously reveals how seriously he took the basic conceptions underlying the Utopian Discourse. In what seems like an echo of that Discourse he excoriates pride, makes its subjection one of the chief ends of education, and prescribes a particular course of reading as a specific against it: "The more I see the difficulty of getting rid of this pest of pride, the more do I see the necessity of getting to work at it from childhood. For I find no other reason why this evil clings to our hearts, than because almost as soon as we are born it is sown in the tender minds of children by their nurses, it is cultivated by their teachers, and brought to its full growth by their parents. . . . That this plague of vainglory may be banished far from my children, I do desire that you, my dear Gonnell, and their mother and all their friends would sing this song to them and repeat it and beat it into their heads—that vainglory is a thing despicable and to be spit upon. . . . To this nothing will more conduce than to read to them the lessons of the ancient Fathers, who, they know, cannot be angry with them; and as they honor them for their sanctity, they must needs be much moved by their authority."

From the letter to Gonnell and the Utopian Discourse we can epitomize More's views on education. Broadly considered, education is the means by which good Christians and good citizens are made, and therefore a good society maintained. From childhood on man is formed by the institutions—the pattern of culture, to use present-day jargon—amid which he is reared, and by the specific precept and instruction of his family and his teachers. Such instruction must include both moral indoctrination and learning in the more technical sense, but to treat the two as separate is wrong since proper training in the humanities is itself one of the best kinds of moral indoctrination. In the best society institutions and instruction work together to destroy pride, the worst bane of man and his world. Thus it is in Utopia. But in the sick degenerate society of sixteenth century Christendom, whose institutions instead of controlling vainglory exalt it, the burden of the suppression of pride falls on instruction, on education in the narrower sense.

Thus in More's view the calling of the educator is among the noblest a man can follow. In the Good Society he assigns the work of teaching to the priests, the most highly honored men in Utopia.[19] In the Europe of his own day education was the calling of the men More held most dear and respected most profoundly, the Christian humanists. Some, like Grocyn and Linacre and Lilly, were teachers in the direct and conventional sense. Some founded or brought about the founding of great schools of the New Learning and dedicated their efforts and fortunes to the maintenance and improvement of those schools—Budé with the Collège de France, Busleyden with the College of Three Tongues at Louvain, and More's spiritual mentor Colet with St. Paul's School. Some, like Vives, served for a time as tutors to the great. All to some degree, but preeminently the greatest of them all, Erasmus, were the teachers of the teachers of northern Europe, not so much through formal instruction but through their writings. Erasmus wrote new grammars and revised and translated old ones, composed "Institutions" for great princes, manuals for Christian knights, and handbooks for the guidance of youth. In the *Colloquies* he combined in a pleasant single dose instruction in sound Latinity and indoctrination in sound morals. But short of a complete catalogue of his works and translations no statement can do justice to the extent and pertinacity of his pedagogic labors. For from about 1500 on, practically every literary enterprise he engaged in had a didactic motive: the translation of pagan Greeks and the Greek Fathers, the editions of Latin authors, the collection of Jerome's letters, the commentaries on Scripture, the collections of adages, even—or perhaps most of all—the *Novum Instrumentum*, the translation of the New Testament. It is hardly too much to say that More regarded the educational work of his beloved Erasmus and the other Christian humanists as the most important work being done in Europe in his day.

If we ask how the Christian humanist who avoids court

[19] L 284, E 106, C 131-132

service and remains an unattached intellectual serves the *Res Publica Christiana,* here we have the answer. He nobly serves the Christian commonwealth by educating it, either directly in a school or indirectly by the propagation of good learning and right living through his writings. Nor can a man hope to make the best of both worlds—both to educate Christendom and to serve one of its princes. Erasmus knew this very well; when his friend More announced his final capitulation to Henry VIII he replied ruefully, "You will be taking service under an excellent prince; but there is no doubt that you will be carried away from us and from learning."[20] For a royal councilor the time given to the education of Christendom could only be what was left over after the prince's demands were met, and the demands of Renaissance princes on their servants being what they were, it was sure to be a slim remainder. But that was not all of it, or the worst of it. True teaching needs free speaking, and never more than in a sick society. But in some matters the lips of a royal councilor are sealed, and in others his words are not unsuspect since his voice has been bought and paid for by his prince. He cannot oppose in the forum the policies adopted in his presence at the council board, and he must form his phrases to the will of the earthly master that he is bound by oath to serve. He may become a ruler in a realm; he can no longer be the educator of Christendom. "If I would speak such things that be true, I must needs speak such things," cries Hythloday at the end of the Dialogue of Counsel.[21] It is the cry of the unattached intellectual, the Christian humanist, the free teacher of Europe.

In uncovering the positive alternative for a Christian humanist to service in a prince's council we may have found, too, the solution to a problem that we have left open for a long while now, the problem of why More offered no guidance

[20] N 3:369; A 3:829, lines 4-6 [21] L 100, E 42, C 41

or advice to lead Europe from its evil ways to the best state of the commonwealth. Like the other great Christian humanists, More was an educator, and when he wrote the Utopian Discourse he was still a free intellectual. Now as the humanists saw it, the duty of a teacher was to set forth the ideal standard in all things as an example, a challenge, and a rebuke to the world. Thus they did not write about fairly good rulers and moderately decent aristocrats and reasonably viable governments; they set forth the image of the perfect prince and the ideal Christian knight—and the best state of the commonwealth. They did not believe such exercises were futile. The faith of the pedagogue, especially of the innovating reforming pedagogue, was strong in the Christian humanists: faith in the saving power of words. They were sustained in their efforts by an abiding trust that mere verbal utterance, effectively arranged, appropriately varied, and frequently repeated, does indeed actually perform work in the world, that the Idea of the Good through the Word does in truth become Flesh in the daily acts of men's daily lives.

Now if truth unaided except by its enunciation is truly efficacious, then it is the obligation of the follower of truth to enunciate it, and in so doing he fulfills his highest duty. And this holds of the truth about society, about "the best state of a commonwealth," as well as of the truth about God; indeed those truths are ultimately one. And so having set forth the best state of the commonwealth in *Utopia*, the Christian humanist More was not at all bound to lay roads and propose means whereby Christian Europe in the sixteenth century could pass from its Slough of Despond to that Blessed Isle. In the Utopian Discourse More had sought to discover the truth and to propagate it in as attractive a form as his command of the essentially pedagogic art of persuasion allowed him. The end was good, the art was good; the philosopher had worked his way to the truth, the artist had set it forth in a garb appropriate to its nobility. As it stood, the Utopian Discourse was a finished work of art and a completed instrument of education. There was nothing left for the philosopher-artist-educator to say or do; from that point on Truth was, as it were, on her own. And so the problem of More's omission from the Discourse section of *Utopia* of expedients for attaining the Good Society is not so much solved as dissolved. It was really never a problem at all. If More had included such expedients, that truly would have been remarkable, that would have called for explanation. His omission of them needs no explanation; it is not remarkable; it is normal; it is precisely what one would expect in a Christian humanist's discourse on the best state of a commonwealth. At least that is what we should expect as long as that humanist remained as securely unattached as More was when he wrote the Utopian Discourse.

6. POWER FOR GOOD

Perhaps it is with Faith and Doubt, Hope and Despair, as it has been said to be with Love and Hate, that at its point of highest intensity each comes closest to the other. In the case of Erasmus, that Christian humanist exemplar of the unattached and innovating intellectual, this was certainly true. His hopes that he might make the truth prevail merely by teaching and preaching it often gave place to the blackest despair as to the efficacy of mere words, and his faith that he might persuade the world to alter its ways gave place to doubt whether all his labors for a brave, new, and reasonable world had changed the course of the wicked old world a jot or a tittle. In his moments of doubt and despair he was but suffering the inevitable lot of the unattached intellectual innovator. Rarely can such men altogether free themselves from the persistent and ungentle ministrations of a *Doppel-*

ganger, who measures the state of things as the innovators envisage them against the state of things as they are, and notes the peculiar disparity between their ideal and a reality not perceptibly altered by the spate of words they have poured forth. Faced by the insidious propaganda of the *Doppelganger*, such men must somehow come to terms with the fact that although unattached intellectuals are often quite free to propose innovations, they rarely get a hearing from the men who have the power to put their proposals into execution.

If the unattached intellectual remains an innovator, his only alternative to coming to terms with the above sad fact is to change his situation, to cease to be an unattached intellectual, and to become either a revolutionary or a bureaucrat. And since revolutionary courses commended themselves hardly at all to the Christian humanists, their only real alternative to detachment was entrance into public office where they might seek to win a hearing for their views. From time immemorial many unattached intellectuals have poured forth their censure on their brethren who have deserted to a government career. The no doubt sincere aversion of such men to such a career has been the easier for them to maintain since frequently their own services have not been solicited, and it is not too hard to scorn a way of life to which one has not been invited. For those to whom the opportunity is offered, however, the temptation is exceeding strong. Whatever may be the ultimate source of conscious peaceful social innovation, its main and normal channel runs through the governing body. It is imposed by men with the authority or power to command on men under the obligation or necessity of obeying. On men like the Christian humanists whose words for years had won approbation and acclaim but who had never had the pleasure of seeing the grammar of assent eventuate in even a brief chapter of coherent action, the magic of the imperium that could transform their precepts into edicts binding on all must have exerted a peculiar and strong attraction.

The magnetic effect was doubtless increased by the ease with which the doors of political preferment swung wide for the apostles of the New Learning. In increasing number from 1500 on, the humanists received invitations to enter the service of the rulers of Western Europe. This is not the place to investigate the details of their absorption into the councils of princely governments. Although education in the humanities was never to displace education in law as a line of access to office, it did provide a viable alternative route to preferment by the middle of the second decade of the sixteenth century; and it had become desirable for ambitious men everywhere at least to profess sympathy with the educational doctrines of the humanists.

Although all the courts of Europe were turning unwonted attention to the hiring, care, and feeding of impecunious men of letters, in no court had the absorption of humanists into the royal service gone further than in England. There a king, himself something of an adept in the New Learning, in the first ten years of his reign so festooned his court with Christian humanists as to become the admiration of Erasmian circles. Erasmus himself spoke of Henry's court as "the seat and citadel of the best studies and of the highest characters ... where under princely favor good letters are dominant ... and a sentence of banishment has been passed against that futile and tasteless learning with its masked affectation of holiness, which used to be in fashion with uneducated men of education."[1]

7. THE DEBATE ON COUNSEL

And More—the Christian humanist most concerned with

[1] N 3:345; A 3:821, lines 3-9

the kind of reform that could be peacefully achieved only with the authority of the prince to back it—on what grounds could he refuse the opportunity to get a hearing at court for the innovations close to his heart? It was all very well for More, the unattached intellectual of 1515, to speak the truth to the world in the Utopian Discourse and then fold his hands. But in 1516 would he be faithful to his friends, his beliefs, his hopes, himself, if he kept his hands folded when the King pressed on him the chance to deploy his abilities in the place where any acceptance his ideas gained would be reflected promptly in the constitution of the English commonwealth?

More well knew that this was the problem, and it was precisely in these terms that he argued it in the Dialogue of Counsel that he wrote in the summer of 1516. There he used the remarks he ascribed to Peter Giles and himself as the vehicle for presenting the case for the participation of the Christian humanist in the counsel of princes, for the entrance of the innovating intellectual into the bureaucracy. The arguments More has Giles make based on self-interest are trivial; it is the argument twice set forth in his own name that carries real force, since it appeals to the Christian humanist on the grounds of duty:

"According to this wisdom . . . of yours . . . apply your wit and diligence to the profit of the weal public, though it be somewhat to your own pain and hindrance. And this shall you never so well do . . . as if you be of some great prince's council, and put into his head . . . honest opinions and virtuous persuasions. For from the prince, as from a perpetual wellspring, cometh among the people the flood of all that is good or evil."[1]

And again: "If you be disposed and can find in your heart to follow some prince's court, you shall with your good coun-

[1] L 37, E 18-19, C 9

sel greatly further and help the commonwealth. Wherefore there is nothing more appertaining to your duty, that is to say to the duty of a good man. For whereas your Plato judgeth that commonwealths shall by this means attain perfect felicity, either if philosophers be kings, or else if kings give themselves to the study of philosophy, how far I pray you shall commonwealths then be from this felicity, if philosophers will vouchsafe to instruct kings with their good counsel?"[2]

Hythloday does not shrink from this argument but meets it head on by imaginatively reconstructing the effect that the advice of a free-speaking Christian humanist would have if it were offered to a Christian prince of his day. Suppose, he says, that he was to take a place in the council of the King of France, meeting in that King's very presence. The councilors "beat their brains and search the very bottoms of their wits to discuss by what craft and means the king may still keep Milan and draw to him again fugitive Naples, and then how to conquer the Venetians, and how to bring under his jurisdiction all Italy, then how to win the dominion of Flanders, Brabant, and of all Burgundy: with diverse other lands whose kingdoms he hath long ago in mind and purpose invaded."[3] One after another then the councilors propose devices, each promising a measure of success for the ends in view, each commensurate with the others in the abysmal hypocrisy, fraud, chicanery, brutality, bad faith and general all-around viciousness of the means suggested for the attainment of those ends.[4]

Suppose then, says Hythloday, "I should declare unto them that all this busy preparance to war, whereby so many nations for his sake should be brought into a troublesome hurly-burly, when all his coffers were emptied, his treasures wasted and his people destroyed, should at length through some mis-

[2] L 79-80, E 34, C 30-31
[3] L 81-82, E 35, C 31
[4] L 82-84, E 35-36, C 31-32

chance be in vain and to no effect: and that therefore, it were best for him to content himself with his own Kingdom of France, as his forefathers and predecessors did before him, to make much of it to enrich it and to make it as flourishing as he could, to endeavor himself to love his subjects, and again to be beloved of them, willing to live with them, peaceably to govern them, and with other kingdoms not to meddle, seeing that which he hath already is even enough for him, yea and more than he can well turn him to."[5] Suppose again that the subject of the conference was not foreign but domestic affairs, and that "some king and his council were together whetting their wits and devising what subtle craft they might invent to enrich the king with great treasures of money."[6] Again the councilors propose devices, again the devices promise a measure of success for the end in view, again each device is commensurate with the others in the abysmal hypocrisy, fraud, chicanery, brutality, bad faith, and general all-around viciousness of the means suggested for the attainment of the ends.[7] Suppose at this juncture, Hythloday continues, "I should rise up and boldly affirm that all these counsels be to the king's dishonor and reproach, whose honor and safety is more and rather supported and upholden by the wealth and riches of his people than by his own treasures . . . and that . . . the king ought to take more care for the wealth of the people than for his own wealth, even as the office and duty of a shepherd is, in that he is a shepherd, to feed his sheep rather than himself."[8]

If he were to render such advice, Hythloday implies, he would only verify experimentally what he already knew well enough—that a Christian humanist is not brought into the councils of a prince to offer his advice against the courses that that prince wants to follow. Such advice, More remarks,

[5] L 87, E 37, C 34
[6] L 88, E 37, C 34
[7] L 88-92, E 37-39, C 34-36
[8] L 92-93, E 39, C 37

"would be heard, . . . God help me, not very thankfully,"[9] and the humanist who spoke thus would find out that he was getting as little hearing for his innovations from the mighty by being inside their councils as he got before when he was outside them as an unattached intellectual. Indeed, a humanist who kept on proposing such innovations in those councils would likely soon find himself an unattached intellectual again, willingly or perforce.

Now in his role of devil's advocate in the Dialogue, More does not attempt to evade the powerful objection that Hythloday has raised to submitting Christian humanists to "the bondage of kings." He offers his answer in a long passage so remarkable that we must describe it rather fully. For such advice as Hythloday has just proposed to give to princes he would find only "deaf hearers, doubtless," More retorts, "and in good faith no marvel." It is neither proper nor permissible for an adviser to give advice that he is "sure shall never be regarded nor received. For how can such strange informations be profitable, or how can they be beaten into their heads whose minds be already prevented with clean contrary persuasions." Such idle talk is mere "school philosophy . . . which thinketh all things meet for every place," and it indeed has no place in the councils of the great. There is another philosophy more civil, however, that knows its own role, and "ordering and behaving herself in the play that she hath in hand, playeth her part accordingly with comeliness, uttering nothing out of due order and fashion, and this is the philosophy that you must use. . . . Whatsoever part you have taken upon you, play that as well as you can and make the best of it. And do not therefore disturb and bring out of order the whole matter because that another which is merrier and better cometh to your remembrance. So the case standeth in a commonwealth, and so it is in the consultations of kings and princes. If evil

[9] L 87, E 37, C 34

opinions and naughty persuasions cannot be utterly and quite plucked out of their hearts, if you cannot even as you would remedy vices, which use and custom hath confirmed, yet for this cause you must not leave and forsake the commonwealth; you must not forsake the ship in the tempest because you cannot rule and keep down the winds. No, nor you must not labor to drive into their heads new and strange informations, which you know well shall be nothing regarded with them that be of clean contrary minds. But you must with a crafty wile and a subtle train study and endeavor yourself as much as in you lieth to handle the matter wittily and handsomely for the purpose, and that which you cannot turn to good, so to order it that it be not very bad."[10]

The passage is notable on several counts, and most obviously for its open-eyed realism. The author of *Utopia* was no Utopian. He knew that the intellectual in a bureaucracy has little chance to innovate, that the mere presence of Christian humanists in princely councils afforded neither the assurance nor even the hope that the aspirations of the Christian humanists might shortly and fully be realized. He knew that in such councils a man must temper his speech, and that if he must always speak the truth as he saw it he had no place there. Yet despite this insight into the frustration which Christian humanists were certain to suffer in princely councils—perhaps rather because of this insight—More presents a lively, cogent, and persuasive case for their entry into such councils.

In this respect the passage is unique in *Utopia*. It is full, it is carefully argued, it is highly coherent, it is vehement and tinged with a strong moral conviction. Up to this point all the coherence, vehemence, and moral conviction have been on Hythloday's side. And after this point, in the scant five pages remaining before More wrote finis to his book, the scales are again weighted in Hythloday's favor. Set any of the other

[10] L 98-100, E 41-42, C 39-41

arguments that More ascribes to himself against those he ascribes to Hythloday, and the disparity in their quality and conviction is unmistakable. Set this one argument against all that Hythloday says in opposition to the involvement of the intellectual in a bureacracy, and although the positions maintained are irreconcilable, they are so evenly matched that it is impossible to tell on the face of them which represented More's own belief at the time he wrote. For once, and only for once, Hythloday gets paid back in coin as good as he gave.

8. WHAT MORE DID

This very shrewd defense of the duty of the Christian humanist to render counsel provided the foundation for the earliest formulation of the hypothesis that in *Utopia* More's own convictions are expressed in the arguments he ascribes to himself.[1] Although we have seen this notion collapse when applied to More's defense of private property,[2] it is still at least possible that in the case of counsel the argument that More ascribes to himself is the one he really believes to be true. It is possible; is it true? In this particular instance do the arguments More puts in his own mouth represent his actual conviction at the time he wrote? Since, as I have observed, there is little to choose between the two sides of the debate on counsel as he presents them in the Dialogue, we must look elsewhere than to the book for an answer to our question; we must examine the course of More's own career around this time.

Wishing to publish some letters he had written to More, Erasmus sent his English servant John Smith to London to pick them up in March 1518.[3] John got back from London a

[1] Chambers, p. 155
[2] See above, Part Two, sections 1 and 2.
[3] N 3:288; A 3:785, lines 1-5

little before April 17.[4] On that day Erasmus wrote William Nesen, "More . . . is now quite a courtier, always attending on the King, whose secretary he is."[5] It is quite clear from his note to Nesen that in a letter not preserved, or from a word-of-mouth message borne by the messenger John Smith, Erasmus received at this time his first notification of his friend's decision to enter the service of Henry VIII. His correspondence for the few days following Smith's return attests to the fact that he had no earlier inkling of what More intended to do. His letters are full of the news. He adverts to it in no less than five of them. Besides announcing the change to Nesen, he writes Tunstall, "I should deplore the fortune of More in being enticed into a court, if it were not under such a king, and with so many learned men for companions and colleagues, it may seem not a court but a temple of the Muses."[6] We may be sure that his letters to Pace and to Henry VIII written at the same time and full of praise for a court at once "the seat and citadel of the best studies and of the highest characters" where "the greatest favor and the highest authority are accorded to those who most excel in learning and integrity of life"[7]—we may be sure that these letters indicate Erasmus' reaction to the news of More's decision and in part his attempt to reconcile himself with it. To More himself Erasmus wrote, "As to your being attached to the court, there is one thing that consoles me; you will be taking service under an excellent prince. But there is no doubt that you will be carried away from us and from literature."[8]

Erasmus had every reason to be surprised, at least if all his correspondence with More during the preceding months has survived. In the previous September More was at Calais on

[4] N 3:342; A 3:816, lines 2-6 [5] *ibid.*
[6] N 3:361; A 3:832, lines 35-37
[7] N 3:345, 367-368; A 3:821, lines 1-2, 834, lines 12-13
[8] N 3:369; A 3:829, lines 4-6

his second mission for the King. Again the commercial interests of the City were much concerned in the treaty being negotiated, so no more than the first mission does this second one indicate any commitment on his part to enter permanently into the royal service. Still Erasmus was anxious. He wrote More, "I have received a commission on the part of the Emperor about some matters of importance, but shall do anything rather than become entangled in that kind of business; and how glad I should be if you were clear!"[9] This has all the earmarks of an epistolary gambit, since nothing in the relations of Erasmus with the Emperor suggests that such a commission was likely, Erasmus does not mention it in any other letter, and no evidence of its existence has ever been discovered.[10]

If reassurances as to More's intentions were what Erasmus was seeking, he got them very shortly. On October 25 More wrote him, "I approve of your plan in not wishing to be involved in the busy trifles of princes; and you show your love for me by desiring that I may be disentangled from such matters, in which you can scarcely believe how unwillingly I am engaged. Nothing indeed can be more hateful to me than my present mission. I am sent to stay at a little seaport with a disagreable soil and climate; and whereas at home I have the greatest abhorrence of litigation, even when it brings me profit, you may imagine what annoyance it must cause me here when it comes accompanied with loss."[11] With such a letter in hand and no later notice from More that he had had a change of heart,[12] it is hardly to be wondered at that Erasmus was bowled over by the news that John Smith brought back from London in April.

[9] N 3:70; A 3:669, lines 12-14 [10] A 3:669, line 12, note

[11] N 3:103; A 3:688, lines 13-21

[12] The only letter More wrote Erasmus in the interim gives no indication of a change. N 3:131-134; A 3:706

All this enables us to date at least roughly the time when More did make his fateful decision. In view of his October letter to Erasmus it is hard to believe that he made up his mind to enter the King's service while he was still tasting the miseries of that service as he experienced it at Calais. He did not get back to England, however, until about Christmas. On the other hand, when he wrote his defense of Greek studies to the University of Oxford late in March he was probably already committed, since the letter came from Abington where the court had gone in flight from the plague, and in it More speaks like one with authority and not as a scribe.[13] Somewhere in the first three months of 1518, then, More made up his mind to join the court. Thus at least seventeen months and perhaps twenty months elapsed between the writing of the Dialogue of Counsel and More's entry into the royal service. During that time he was being pulled toward it by Henry and Wolsey and, if we may accept one of his later yarns as autobiographical, pushed toward it by his wife. If he was convinced when he wrote the Dialogue that given the opportunity a Christian humanist ought to go into the council of a great prince, it is hard to see why he did not go there. The door was open; many of his dearest friends had already passed through it; the only one that was holding him back was himself. He was not likely to be holding himself back for any material or personal reason; he did not allow such reasons to determine the grave decisions of his life. I can only conclude from what lies on the face of the evidence that for about a year and a half after he wrote the Dialogue of Counsel he did not enter the royal service because he did not think he ought to be there, because he suspected he ought not to be there. And if that is so, his own attitude on the bondage of princes when he wrote the Dialogue of Counsel is the same as the one there expressed by Hythloday and is not the one that

[13] Rogers, no. 60

he ascribes to himself. At that time he had not convinced himself even by his own brilliant argument that the Christian humanist innovator was in duty bound to become a royal servant, that in so doing he would most nearly achieve his own highest purpose. In 1516 More still tenaciously clung to the position of the unattached intellectual of which Erasmus' career was the exemplar.

9. THE ANSWER IN THE DIALOGUE

In the face of his own scintillating job of devil's advocacy, why did More remain unconvinced that it was his duty to enter Henry VIII's service in 1516? In doing that job he had succeeded in cutting much of the ground of resistance from under his own feet. As devil's advocate he gave up the position, naïvely taken at the outset, that merely by whispering good and virtuous advice into the prince's ear the Christian humanist was going to convert him into a paragon of all virtues, that mere monition would transform into apostles of sweetness and light the hardened practitioners of *realpolitik* who everywhere dominated the royal councils. But More gave up this advanced and untenable position, typical of an unadulterated Christian humanism, only to make an orderly retreat to a far stronger position, better suiting a Christian humanist who was also a statesman-like realist. In the council of a prince a man like Hythloday or More would indeed have to abjure the kind of free irresponsible talk that he could indulge in as an unattached intellectual, as well as any overwrought notions that he might entertain about directing the course of policy. But if he is willing to do that, if he will discipline his tongue, if he will subject himself to the restraint and learn the civil manners that he must display as a councilor, he can in his capacity of royal adviser do the commonwealth substantial service by wisely tempering ill matters until they become, if not wholly good, yet less bad than they were. And this is no trifling thing, since the matters of a prince are life and death to his subjects, and in procuring even a small deflection of policy from an evil course, that would not have been procured had he not persuaded to it, the Christian humanist councilor can ease the burdens of many of the oppressed.

Hythloday's answer to the devil's advocate is that he is misconstruing what necessarily happens in a prince's council and evading the moral implications of that kind of service for the Christian humanists themselves. Men are called into a prince's service only to help the prince work out expeditious ways for getting what he is determined already to have at any cost. Instead of leading him along paths that they believe to be good, they soon find that they are having their brains picked to ease his way along paths they know to be bad. Such talents as they have end up by being deployed not to support but to subvert the causes closest to their hearts. As Hythloday says, he "truly would prevail" little in the councils of a king, "*for I must either give a different opinion from the rest there, and for what good that would do, I had as well give no opinion at all; or I must give the same opinion as they,*[1] and . . . help to further their madness."[2] Once inside the royal council a man must learn to disregard the possibilities not set before him, and merely take his pick among those that are. The innovating intellectual who surrenders his freedom to define the problem and ends up by merely giving those in power advice on the handiest way to follow a predetermined course of action cannot evade responsibility for what he is doing. Willy-nilly what he does is to lend "his skills and knowledge

[1] "For other I must say other ways then they say, and then I were as good to say nothing; or else I must say the same that they say"; *Nam aut diuersa sentiam, quod perinde fuerit ac si nihil sentiam; aut eadem, et ipsorum adiutor sim.*

[2] L 102, E 42-43, C 42

to the preservation of a given type of institutional arrangement,"[3] of which he presumably disapproves. He cannot evade this necessity. He will be called on not to temporize but to assent with the show of enthusiasm deemed appropriate to a king's servant. For a circle of royal councilors "is no place to dissemble in, nor to wink in. Naughty counsels must be openly allowed, and very pestilent decrees must be approved."[4] In the end he will do little or nothing to better the commonwealth, but will himself be corrupted by the corrupt atmosphere he breathes. "A man can have no occasion to do good, chancing into the company of them which will sooner make naught a good man than be made good themselves." At the very best, if he is not spiritually defiled, he will be blamed for the foulness of his fellows; "if he remain good and innocent, yet the wickedness and folly of others shall be imputed to him and laid on his neck."[5]

10. THE FATEFUL DECISION

Such was the ultimate conclusion at the bottom of More's probings into the problem of counsel, such was his final answer in theory and practice—in 1516. Two years later More was a royal pensioner, a royal councilor, secretary to His Majesty the King.[1] And this brings us to the last problem about *Utopia* that we will attempt to solve. Is there anywhere in that book a clue to what led More to change his mind? Having argued himself into one position in 1516, how had he managed to argue himself out of it and into another and opposite position by 1518? We have already seen that the considerations of interest that were in his mind when he wrote Erasmus about the King's offer were given short shrift

[3] Merton, p. 411 [4] L 103, E 43, C 42 [5] *ibid.*

[1] Routh, p. 92, note 3

in the Dialogue of Counsel.[2] From the time he wrote that Dialogue, his position on the question of counsel must be regarded not as the result of external pressures and inducements, but as the consequence of moral conviction, and therefore the change in More's position between 1516 and 1518 must be ascribed to a change of conviction. It seems to me dubious psychology to suggest that a man of More's temper, having pushed beyond considerations of interest to considerations of principle, could have then reverted to interest as a decisive element in his choice, that having already plumbed the moral depths of the problem of counsel he could have settled it in his own case on grounds of expediency.

Nor can I lend much credence to the notion that More was forced into the royal service through either fear or unbearable pressure of an unspecified nature exercised by the King and the Cardinal. Various modern authors have read this meaning into Roper's account of the motives of More's decision,[3] and into Erasmus' and More's own reiterated assertions of his reluctance, to enter the King's council. The evidence here does not seem to me capable of sustaining the construction put upon it. In the first place there is, to my knowledge, no proof at all that Henry VIII or any other Tudor ever overtly or covertly punished, threatened to punish, or tried to punish any subject of theirs for evading a high post in their service.[4] And even assuming the will to do so, it is hard to imagine what pretext the King could have found for punishing a man like More, whose personal life was so exemplary and whose personal fortune was so little dependent on royal favor. As to the unbearable pressures of an unspecified nature it is hard to imagine what they might have been, unless under that evil-

[2] See above Part Three, section 4. [3] Roper, p. 10

[4] Reginald Pole might be regarded as an exception to this rule; but Henry wanted Pole back in England for sinister reasons having nothing to do with the royal service.

sounding rubric we include the persistent offers of a post and the successively higher bids of a material nature that More received from the court. But we have already seen reasons to doubt whether More would have sold himself into bondage to a king at any price calculable in pecuniary terms. It is finally beyond belief that, given the will, a resourceful man like More could evade for only two years a position of the kind that under scarcely less pressure, with no greater aversion to the court way of life, with less political ingenuity and political convictions less firmly grounded, Erasmus succeeded in evading all his life. If More declined to enter the royal service in 1516, it was because he thought he ought not enter; when he did enter in 1518, it was because he thought he ought to enter.

This conclusion is in no way inconsistent with More's frequent private expressions of his feeling about the royal service.[5] The feeling expressed is one of unqualified and unlimited distaste, and there is no reason to doubt that More is absolutely sincere in what he so consistently says on this subject. He not only had a distaste for court life by anticipation before he came to court; he seems never to have conquered his aversion for it throughout his public career.[6] The court's pompousness, its ceremony and protocol, all the tabus that for good reason surround the source of political power long after the naked primitive sense of *mana* has appropriated a more civilized garb, all this apparently nauseated More. The formality and artificiality of court life and manners only made him yearn the more impatiently for the easy natural comradeship of his family in Chelsea. His strong feelings on this score led to a curious bit of byplay when to escape to his family from a king too taken with the charm of his com-

[5] See above, Part Three, section 8.

[6] See Roper's account of More's surrender of the Chancellorship; Roper, pp. 53-54.

panionship, More, one of the wittiest men of his time, sat about for days on end being stupid in order to bore Henry into letting him go home for dinner.[7] Granted this revulsion to court life, the fact remains that while in one sense More never overcame it, in another sense he had already overcome it when he wrote the Dialogue of Counsel. If that Dialogue indicates anything at all about More's attitude, it indicates that he felt that the question, "to serve, or not to serve," could be answered by a Christian humanist only on the basis of duty and obligation, *not* on the basis of his own personal tastes and appetites. Either More had conquered his purely personal aversion to court service without by any means annihilating it when he wrote the Dialogue of Counsel, or the Dialogue, written when the problem it dealt with was of immense concern to its author, is a mere irrelevant rhetorical exercise. Since the latter alternative seems not altogether likely, we must conclude that the King had need neither of threats nor of unspecified pressures to overcome More's personal predilections since More had himself already overcome them. We are forced to look then for a change in More's principles or for a change of circumstances of such a nature as to lead him to believe that those principles had ceased to be relevant in his case.

Now to the best of my knowledge neither More's correspondence at this time nor his later writings give us any clue as to what induced him to reverse his decision. And so we are thrown back on the Dialogue of Counsel, which is after all the fullest exposition he ever made of his views on the question of the public duties of a Christian humanist. Yet this may seem a rather unpromising place to seek for the clue we want. We have just seen reason to believe that More's own opinion was expressed in Hythloday's final argument against the entry of a Christian humanist into the royal service. He

[7] Roper, pp. 11-12

makes the point so effectively that he seems to be stuck with it, and we should hardly expect to find in the Dialogue of Counsel the lever for getting him unstuck. Oddly enough there is such a lever, and it is in the very speech in which Hythloday seems to settle the matter once and for all. Before putting the clincher on his argument, he tries to dispose of the jibe that all his fine proposals for reform are mere school philosophy, well enough in idle conversation among friends, but quite inappropriate to a king's council where serious matters are discussed. There might be some justice in that jibe, he says, if he had proposed that "all things be common" as they were in Utopia. But he proposed no such thing, and as to what he had advocated, "I cannot see why it should seem strange or foolishly new-fangled. . . . What was in my communication contained that might not and ought not in any place to be spoken? Saving that to them which have thoroughly decreed and determined with themselves to run headlong the contrary way it cannot be acceptable and pleasant, because it calleth them back and showeth them the jeopardies."[8]

Hythloday's protest is well justified. Up to this point in the Dialogue of Counsel he has mentioned many things which he would feel obliged to advise a prince to do or refrain from doing. Some of that advice might be unpalatable to a ruler, but it is by no means radical. It has nothing whatever to do with the community of living practiced in Utopia, which indeed to this moment Hythloday has not mentioned. Now More had in fact already written the Utopian Discourse with its panegyric of a community of living, and it is important to note the distinct implication here that as a royal councilor he would not feel bound to advise the prince to model his realm on the Utopian commonwealth. This does not mean that he was merely joking in the Utopian Discourse or that he did not intend it to be taken seriously. It does mean that as a

[8] L 100-101, E 42, C 41

hard-headed realist he did not for a moment think that he could bring the Utopian social order into being by serving in a royal council. When he wrote the Utopian Discourse as an unattached intellectual, he was rendering society the only service an unattached intellectual can render it. Over against the policies pursued by all the rulers of Christendom and against the existing social order, he was establishing a set of alternatives, imperishably recorded, to show that there was another and a better way than the way those rulers followed, and a not impossible state of the commonwealth better than any existing commonwealth. But he did not believe that any prince of his day would seek to establish such a commonwealth. Nor did he believe that a humanist in a prince's council was bound to persuade him to make the attempt.

What More believed a Christian humanist was bound to advise a sixteenth century prince to do is stated or implied in the Dialogue of Counsel. It is contained in the invectives against enclosure,[9] idle retainers,[10] and the merciless punishment of petty crime;[11] in the advice Hythloday says he would feel impelled to give a king contemplating a war of conquest or the fiscal oppression of his subjects;[12] and in the policies ascribed to the imaginary realms of the Polylerites,[13] the Macarians,[14] and the Achorians.[15] The advice falls under the general heads of foreign policy, fiscal policy, and domestic policy.

On the first two heads we find the essence of what a humanist adviser would be bound to tell his prince in Hythloday's polemics against wars of conquest and against ruthless royal fiscalism, from which we have already quoted. These polemics he reinforces with his tales of the Achorians and the

[9] L 51-54, E 23-25, C 15-18
[10] L 45-47, E 21-22, C 13
[11] L 43-44, 58; E 20-21, 26; C 11-12, 19
[12] L 84-87, 92-95; E 36-37, 39-40; C 32-34, 37-38
[13] L 64-71, E 28-31, C 22-26
[14] L 95-97, E 36-37, C 33-34
[15] L 84-87, E 40, C 38-39

Macarians. When the Achorians felt the burdensome consequences to themselves of a conquest they had won for their prince, they were so little disposed to feed his greed for glory that they gave him his choice to rule over them and give up his conquest or to forsake them and rule his newly-won dominion, on the grounds that he could not truly do right to both realms at once.[16] The Macarians, to prevent their king from piling up a great treasure with which to plague foreign peoples or his own subjects, had enacted that he might not at any time have more than a thousand pounds in his treasury.[17]

More's concern with the foreign and fiscal policy of the rulers of Europe is really subordinate to his concern with their domestic policy. For the most evil consequence of the lust for domination and the insatiable appetite for riches of the prince is the insupportable burdens they inflict on the people, and especially on the poor. These miserable creatures are crushed with taxes for the prince's wars, and when the wars are over they are pillaged by a soldiery that has lost its aptitude for everything but violence. Then driven by penury resulting from the folly of war, or worse, by mere avarice, the ruler resurrects obsolete laws, invents bad new ones, and sells immunity from both, intimidates judges to pervert justice, and employs all the resources of force and fraud at his disposal to squeeze yet more wealth from his exhausted people —the shepherd turned vampire sucking the blood of his own sheep. These sins of commission of Christian princes cried to heaven for amendment, and More believed that no councilor could be silent in the face of them and retain his integrity. And there were sins of omission equally black—the fruit of the sloth, callousness, indifference, and ignorance of the ruler. For the prince is bound to do more than refrain from harassing his weaker subjects himself; he must protect them from

[16] L 95-97, E 36-37, C 33-34

[17] L 84-87, E 40, C 38-39

the oppression of others. The most eloquent invective of the Dialogue of Counsel is spent on the mighty and rich oppressors of the poor and humble. Who are these oppressors? They are the idle gentlemen and noblemen, who rack-rent their tenants to support a wastrel rout of retainers, and when the retainers grow old turn them out doors and into vagrancy.[18] They are the enclosers—"noblemen and gentlemen, yea, and certain abbots," who run sheep where men once tilled the soil, "and turn all dwelling places and all glebeland into desolation and wilderness," driving out the husbandmen, "poor, silly, wretched souls, men, women, husbands, wives, fatherless children, widows, woeful mothers with their young babes, and their whole household small in substance and much in number."[19] They are the graziers engrossing the wool in what if it is not "*a monopoly . . . is surely an oligopoly*,"[20] and driving the clothmakers out of work.[21] Such are the men who squeeze the poor to the point of desperation, and then to thieving, and then hang the miserable wretches under the guise of laws which, as More had already written, are merely "the unjust dealings" of the rich, falsely by them called justice.[22] Such are the men who drive the oppressed "to this extreme necessity, first to steal and then to die."[23]

Here as usual More not only went to the root of the evil; he also worked out the remedy not in vague general terms, but specifically and clearly. The remedy must come from the king, and it must be administered with the full force of the government behind it. "Make a law," More writes, "that they which plucked down farms and towns of husbandry shall build them up again or else yield and uprender the possession of them to such as will go to the cost of building them anew.

[18] L 45-47, E 21-22, C 13
[19] L 51-54, E 23-24, C 15-17
[20] L 55, *Si monopolium appelari non potest . . . certe oligopolium est.* Omitted by Robinson.
[21] L 54-55, E 24-25, C 17
[22] L 303, E 112, C 140
[23] L 44, E 21, C 12

Suffer not these rich men to buy up all, to engross and forestall, and with their monopoly to keep the market alone as please them. Let not so many be brought up in idleness, let husbandry and tillage be restored again, let clothworking be renewed, that there may be honest labors for this idle sort to pass their time in profitably, which hitherto . . . poverty has caused to be thieves." Do these things and there will be no need for laws "so hasty to kill a man for taking a little money."[24]

Avoidance of futile and costly wars of continental conquest, renunciation of crooked fiscal devices, a princely and pastoral care for the flock that God entrusted to the ruler to protect it from the ravening and insatiable wolves of the world—these were not Utopian goals, nor were the policies More proposed to attain these ends Utopian policies. They were the minimum that a good Christian was bound to advocate in an English prince's councils, and if he could not advocate at least so much, better had he stay away from such councils altogether.

But if by some turn of fortune there came a time and a place and a prince that made it possible to believe that good counsels would be heard with a welcome ear—what then? Under such circumstances might not the most persistently detached intellectual feel that he should give over his self-imposed isolation from the places of power and seek to further the translation of good intentions into sound policies in the only place where that translation could be made, in the council of the prince? Even as he wrote the Dialogue of Counsel, More might have suspected that the time and the place and the prince were at hand in that year, in his own England, in his own King. By the spring of 1518 his suspicion would have had a chance to grow into a hope, tempered perhaps, but not tempered enough, by a reserve of doubt.

When he came back from the Netherlands, More found

[24] L 57-61, E 25-27, C 18-21

that Thomas Cardinal Wolsey had become beyond dispute the King's first minister, who under Henry and with his good will now exercised undisputed sway over domestic policy as he had for years over foreign policy. It was through his newly acquired office of Chancellor that Wolsey made his influence felt in domestic affairs, and in the hands of that willful, proud, and vigorous man the Chancellor again became in effect what he had been at the zenith of his power in the Middle Ages—the king's secretary of state for all departments. We have seen what More considered the specifications for a sound domestic policy. We may dramatize (without adequately measuring) the impact on him of Wolsey's work in his new office by setting against those specifications a contemporary's account of the social consequences of Wolsey's assumption of the Chancellorship: "By the Cardinal were all men called to account that had the occupying of the King's money in the wars or elsewhere, not to every man's contentation. . . . For a truth he so punished perjury with open punishment . . . that in his time it was less used. He punished also lords, knights, and men of all sorts for riots . . . and maintenance in their countries that the poor men lived quietly, so that no man durst bear for fear of imprisonment, but he himself and his servants were well punished therefor. The poor people perceived that he punished the rich; then they complained without number."[25]

The instruments of Wolsey's action were three courts, none of them courts of common law—Star Chamber, Requests, and Chancery. The last was peculiarly the court of the Chancellor. The first two were staffed by councilors of the King. In the council giving judgment in the Starred Chamber the Chancellor traditionally presided, and where Wolsey presided he also directed. Requests, the court of poor men's causes, had

[25] Edward Hall, *Hall's Chronicle* . . . , ed. H. Ellis, London, 1809, p. 585.

formerly been under the Privy Seal, but when Fox resigned the Keepership in 1516, Wolsey assumed control of that court too. He got his opportunity for action from the premature arteriosclerosis of the common law, a debility that goes far to explain More's contempt for the legal system in which he was trained and by which he had got his living. In the fifteenth century that law had got itself so tangled in technicalities and formalities and so restricted by self-imposed maxims as to reduce itself to impotence in the face of obvious chicanery and overt violence. In an era when after long paralysis the conscience of Europe was beginning to stir again, the common law protested that there was no right unless there was a remedy, and then refused to provide remedies against what the common conscience recognized as grievous wrongs. The law's delays were an effective weapon of aggression in the hands of the rich, who could afford to deploy them, against the poor who could not. In cases so flagrant that mere delay would not suffice, there were always witnesses who could be induced to perjure themselves and bands of armed retainers who could intimidate local juries. So the common law became the happy hunting ground of men rich and powerful enough to acquire the armaments of fraud and thinly veiled force, and against this force and fraud the courts of that law afforded the poor and humble little protection.

Against the rich man's courts of common law Wolsey set the poor man's courts and the "new law of Star Chamber." He did not create Chancery, Requests, and Star Chamber, and he did not invent the devices by means of which those courts drew to themselves cases which hitherto had gone by default for lack of a common law remedy and cases begun at common law whose conclusion there might lead to substantial injustice. But he did infuse those courts with greater vigor than they had ever had before and with greater vigor than the common law courts were to display for many a decade.

Although the bulk of the cases tried in these conciliar courts seem also to have originated in them, intervention in suits already instituted at common law was exasperatingly frequent and exasperatingly effective from the point of view of those who enjoyed the benefits of that law's incompetence. The instruments of this intervention were the injunction and the subpoena. On the basis of what was deemed a reasonable complaint, the conciliar courts would enjoin a plaintiff from proceeding with his case at common law and order him to appear before the king's council ready to answer the complaint or be fined for failure to appear. Once one of these courts had assumed jurisdiction, it elicited evidence by methods which the common law with its antiquated reliance on the juror's knowledge of the fact had never been at pains to devise. The judgment followed quickly thereafter, and the execution hard upon the judgment. Intimidation was impossible since there was no jury to intimidate, the judges were the king's own councilors enjoying his special protection, and it did not occur even to the hardiest noble ruffian to try to scare the advisers of Henry VIII. Of the three conciliar courts Chancery alone seems to have been described at the time as a court of equity, but under Wolsey all three were devoted to seeing to it that justice got done, with, without, or in spite of the common law; and the provision of a recourse beyond common law actions was sure to redound to the advantage of the poor and to the disadvantage of the rich whose abuses had enjoyed a fungoid growth beneath the beneficent shade of time-honored and antiquated forms.

For two years after his return from the Netherlands Thomas More could watch the work of Chancery, Star Chamber, and the Court of Requests. Probably at one time or another he pleaded before all three of them. Equity, the general ideal and purpose of these tribunals, was shortly to be described in the early English defense of it as "an exception of the law of God or the law of reason from the general rules of the law of men, when they by reason of their generality would in any particular case judge against the law of God or the law of reason. . . . Sith the deeds and acts of men for which laws have been ordained happen in divers manners infinitely, it is not possible to make any general rule of law, but that it shall fail in some case; and therefore makers of laws take heed to such things as may often come, and not to every particular case, for they could not though they would. And therefore to follow the words of the law were in some cases against both justice and the commonwealth. . . . A law made by man commanding or prohibiting anything to be done that is against the law of reason or the law of God . . . is no law, but a corruption and manifest error."[26]

With the ideal of equity so expressed, More was certain to sympathize. And he must have been in accord with the principle, on which Wolsey acted, that the King should erect and support courts that would provide justice in instances where the courts of common law failed to do so. With the actual practical work of Wolsey's courts he was bound to be delighted. In their willingness to give hearings without interposing technical impediments, in their direct way of looking for the facts in the case, in their minimizing of court fees they gave the poor such access to justice as they never before had enjoyed. While he encouraged the poor to complain against oppression, Wolsey struck from the hands of the rich and powerful the weapons of oppression. He put out of the council magnates who after the fashion set by the Wars of the Roses were likely to use their influence there to cover their misdoings elsewhere. When England's only Marquess got involved in brawling with other great men, Wolsey hauled him up before Star Chamber and bound him over to good be-

[26] Christopher St. German, *The Doctor and Student*, Cincinnati, 1874, Chapters 16 and 19

havior. He bore down so hard on aristocrats who kept "great flocks of idle and loitering serving men" that the Lord Steward of England and its premier Earl "sent the substance of all my servants to their friends, saving only twelve or sixteen," scarcely enough for respectability much less for intimidation and rioting. Observing these events More might well have been persuaded that far from being "but a certain conspiracy of rich men" the commonwealth of England was being transformed by Wolsey into a certain conspiracy not of but in behalf of poor men, and with this kind of conspiracy he could be heartily in accord. That he was indeed in accord with it, that he thoroughly approved of Wolsey's ends and methods if not of his manner, More clearly revealed a decade later when he himself became Chancellor. Few practices could have rankled more the men who found protection for their abuses in the defects of the common law than Wolsey's use of the injunction to bring the cognizance of their suits into one of his equitable jurisdictions. When the common law judges complained that, as Chancellor, More continued the use of the injunctive procedure, he had a list of the injunctions he had issued drawn up and invited the judges to examine them. After they had done so, "they were all enforced to confess that they in like case could have done no otherwise themselves." He then proposed that "if the justices of every court . . . would upon reasonable considerations by their own discretions, as they were, he thought in conscience bound, mitigate and reform the rigor of the law themselves there should from thenceforth by him no injunctions be granted." When the judges rejected his offer, as he doubtless knew they would, he told them, "forasmuch as yourselves, my lords, drive me to that necessity for awarding out injunctions to relieve the people's injury, you cannot hereafter any more justly blame me."[27] Such a handling of the situation created

[27] Roper, pp. 43-45

by injunctions would have been unimaginable under Wolsey; it was pure More. But the result was that under More and for the rest of the century Wolsey's conciliar courts continued effectively to do the work Wolsey had set them to until the common law reformed itself and until under the Stuarts the Star Chamber became the instrument of royal claims to an arbitrary authority such as no Tudor was so foolish as to make.

Wolsey not only gave hearings at retail to the plaints of the poor against the rich in the conciliar courts, he took the initiative and set out to discover their grievances in the matter in which they were being most cruelly oppressed. In the matter of sheep-running and enclosure he threw the whole force of the royal administration on their side. In 1517 his commissioners of depopulation made an inquest into all enclosures of land made since 1485. Thus for at least twenty-two counties where conversion of arable into pasture had probably been most prevalent the names of the depopulating landlords fell into the hands of Wolsey. The least that can be said for the commissioners is that they sought the facts without respect of persons. The names of petty landlords, new-rich graziers, old gentry, great magnates, court favorites, high officials of church and state, and one of the very commissioners taking the inquest were impartially returned. To estimate the effect of the inquest and Wolsey's subsequent action on it is impossible. We know that he issued a decree ordering the destruction of all enclosures that had been returned as contrary to the statute, but we cannot know how vigorously that decree was executed. We do know that of one hundred and one cases under the decree brought before Chancery on a writ of *supersedeas*, twenty-five received a stay only on condition of compliance within a fixed time, and twenty-five showed that they had already complied. We also know that prosecutions resulting from the inquest continued for years after

Wolsey's fall. But the efficacy of a government's measures against acts contrary to public policy is not measured so much by the number of offenders it punishes as by the number of offenses that by the awe it inspires it prevents from ever taking place. How many would-be depopulators were scared off by Wolsey's "Doomsday of Enclosures" and the action he took against violators of the statutes, there is no means of knowing, nor does the basis for even an educated guess exist. Such a guess would have to be based on a far more exact chronology of the extension of enclosure than any now available or ever likely to be available. All we can say is that the spectacle of even a few hedges being pulled down and houses being rebuilt by landlords at Wolsey's command and their expense may at least have given pause to some prospective investors in hedge planting, house razing, and sheep running.

In any case, in 1516 and 1517 More saw the counsel he would have given his King on domestic policy materializing item for item before his eyes as a government program in being. In the conciliar courts, when he pleaded causes of his clients there, he saw royal councilors—men he knew, his friends—administering the kind of justice he believed in and redressing inequities he detested. But he was neither administering good justice nor redressing manifest inequities; instead he was refusing to take a place offered him beside his friends in the royal council, the one place where the kind of public service he professed to believe in was in fact daily being done by them. More and more the rejection of a position as royal adviser, so strongly stated in the summer of 1516, was hard to maintain; more and more it must have come to seem to him premature and ill-advised, perhaps even petulant and selfish.

Especially so since at the same time More's strictures on royal fiscal policy were becoming irrelevant. After the Parliament of 1515 there was a full stop both to royal extravagance and to royal exactions. From their peak of almost £700,000 in 1513 disbursements of the treasury of the chamber were down nearly to £100,000 in 1516, nearly to £70,000 in 1517, nearly to £50,000 in 1518.[28] There is no evidence of any governmental extortion, and Parliament was not summoned, so there were no new taxes. The reasons for this retrenchment were quite simple. In the Spanish and Tournai campaigns Henry had succeeded in dissipating the mounds of gold that his father had heaped up. In 1515 members of the House of Commons had showed no love for Wolsey or his policies and a considerable truculence about money grants, so the Cardinal was fain to make shift without Parliament. But though a man like More might little respect the motives that impelled Wolsey to three years of retrenchment, he could neither disregard, nor withhold his approbation of, the result.

Perhaps More's acerbity about his mission to Calais may have been born of the vague sense that Wolsey's futile and costly aggressiveness on the continent provided his last thin line of resistance, his last excuse for remaining outside the King's council. But while More was fretting his time away in Calais, this last line of resistance was breaking. Having failed in his best efforts to inveigle somebody, almost anybody, on the continent into waging a war in which he could meddle, Wolsey was ready to wage peace. With his customary aptitude for assuming magnificently positions he could not avoid, he took the generous and noble stance of peace-maker-at-large to Europe. As part of the pacification he induced Henry to cede his conquest of Tournai—all he could show for his father's wasted treasure—to France for an indemnity. England's continental possessions were once more reduced to the port of Calais, and Henry Tudor's feeble attempt to emulate the deeds of Henry of Lancaster was liquidated with

[28] *Letters and Papers of the Reign of Henry VIII*, 2, pp. cxciii-cxciv, 1458-1477.

a fancy flourish that ill concealed the ignominy of its failure. Yet however sordid most of the realities under the tinsel of Wolsey's peace policy, peace itself was one of those realities and the renunciation of continental ambitions, at least for the time being, was another. And peace and renunciation of continental ambitions were the key elements in More's ideal of the right and good foreign policy for England.

One by one the grounds on which Hythloday had based his rejection of the role of royal councilor had been hewn away. The King was laying a heavy hand on rich and powerful oppressors in England; he was cutting the coat of his expenditures to fit the cloth of his revenues and living off his own; he was at peace with the world and no longer engaged in designs of continental conquest. In Henry's council a man who pressed the policies that More believed a Christian humanist was bound to press would only be persuading the King to pursue to the end a path he had already entered. Given the opportunity, could a Christian humanist in good conscience refuse to add his weight to those of others in the council to keep Henry on the course he already seemed inclined to? More evidently felt that he could not. In April 1518 he announced to Erasmus his intention to enter the royal council. In July he accepted an annual pension from the King.

Envoi–The Bitter Fruit

A FEW words only remain to be said about Thomas More and the Dialogue of Counsel in his *Utopia*, and those words are rueful ones. The man who wrote that the king's council was "no place to dissemble in or wink in; naughty counsels must be openly allowed and very pestilent decrees must be approved; he shall be counted worse than a spy, yea almost as evil as a traitor, that with a faint heart doth praise evil and noisesome decrees"; that man, twenty years later bore witness by his death on the scaffold to the wisdom of his own words. In the crisis of England's religious revolution men who had risen as high as More had in the King's service were truly in bondage to a prince; they had lost all their freedom, even the freedom of silence. It was not for what he had said that More died, but for what he had refused to say. He had refused to allow naughty counsels or to approve what he believed to be pestilent decrees; he had stood silent and his silence passed for treason, and so he died.

Yet to More his own death was but the last swallow, and perhaps not the bitterest, in a cup that had long held little but dregs. And before him, after he had downed this last swallow, More firmly believed that there lay eternal glory. A darker day had already passed. Early in the twenties Wolsey could no longer resist the temptation to fish in the bloody pool of continental power politics. He hoped to hook the French crown for his master, an imperial marriage for his master's daughter, and perhaps a papal tiara for his master's zealous and faithful servant. So he launched England, Henry, and himself into a military venture in which none gained anything and all lost a great deal.

In 1523, short of funds to back his megalomaniac speculation in thrones and crowns, Wolsey had Parliament summoned for the first time in eight years and the first time since he had reached indisputable ascendancy in English affairs. He correctly anticipated trouble from a House of Commons unwilling to write blank checks to support a policy of limitless adventuring of which it entirely disapproved. He needed a Speaker of the House to manage its members, soothe their tempers, and induce them to pick the pockets of their constituents to pay for the Cardinal-Archbishop's insatiable appetite for glory. Who better apt for such work than the popular idol, the delight of the City, the proponent of peace, retrenchment, and reform, the author of *Utopia*? In those days the speakership went by assignment from the king, and More received the assignment. He could hardly have had much joy of it, but he performed it manfully, enforcing Wolsey's demands by telling the House that "Of duty men ought not to deny to pay four shillings of the pound." When the session was over More received his reward—£200 and praise for his service in the letter in which the Cardinal solicited the King to pay the money. In "the faithful diligence of the said Sir Thomas More . . . for your subsidy right honorably passed . . . no man could better deserve . . . than he hath done. . . . I am rather moved to put your Highness in remembrance thereof, because he is not the most ready to speak and solicit in his own cause."[1] More was never a ready solicitor in his own cause, but in this particular instance his tongue may have been especially tardy. The future martyr, the saint to be, the author of *Utopia*, the Christian humanist inextricably, wretchedly, unhappily involved in the betrayal and crucifixion of his own most cherished ideals may well have been diffident about asking for those two hundred pounds. To him they may have seemed rather like thirty pieces of silver.

[1] Chambers, 207; *Letters and Papers of the Reign of Henry VIII*, 3, no. 3267.

Appendix A

MORE'S STATE SERVICE BEFORE 1515

There is no evidence whatever that in any ordinary sense of the word More "sought place and wage" under Henry VIII at his accession as suggested by William Nelson, "Thomas More, Grammarian and Orator," *PMLA*, 58, 1943, pp. 347-348, or that he received either before 1518. More's production of a Latin poem at Henry's accession can hardly be so construed. Almost all Englishmen breathed easier at the fall of the regime of Empson and Dudley, and that a leading English literary man should hail the advent to the throne of a prince who was already looked on with high hopes by men of letters was quite natural. The notion that after Henry's accession More "rose rapidly in Crown service" (Ames, p. 42), and that he "was connected with the Crown earlier than has been assumed" (Ames, p. 45) seems to be based on two kinds of evidence, neither of which will bear the interpretation put on it. The first is the traces of More's services on Commission of the Peace, of Array, and of Sewers and in an inquisition *post mortem.* The *omission* of an eminent subject, son of a leading member of the bar, from such Commissions might imply perhaps some special royal disfavor; but the idea that the *presence* of such a man on the Commission of the Peace, much less his selection for the thankless, payless tasks of assembling the county militia and supervising drainage work was a special mark of royal favor would have surprised the numerous recipients of that kind of royal favor among More's contemporaries. The notion that in 1511 "More was already deeply involved in Crown business" (Ames, p. 45) and therefore "connected with the Crown" is based on Ammonius' note of that year assuring Erasmus that More had delivered his letter to Archbishop Warham. More "could scarcely fail to deliver it," Ammonius observes, "since he either speaks to the Archbishop or sees him every day" (N 2:46; Allen 2:243, lines 63-65). Now although More doubtless knew Archbishop Warham, daily personal contact with him would be indeed remarkable were it not for the fact that the Archbishop was also Chancellor, who besides having his own court presided in Star Chamber as well. As we shall see (Part Three, section 2) in the office of Under Sheriff of London since 1510 More almost certainly acted as counsel for the City before both those courts. But at the time of Ammonius' letter, More probably had special occasion frequently to be with, if not always to speak to, the Archbishop. The Merchants of the Staple were engaged in a long-winded suit against the Merchant Adventurers. The case was being heard in Star Chamber in 1511 (Georg Schanz, *Englische Handelspolitik gegen Ende des Mittelalters*, 2 vols., Leipzig, 1881, II, 555-565). Apparently More was among the counsel for the Staplers in the suit (*Acts of Court of the Mercers' Company, 1453-1527*, ed. L. Lyell and F. D. Watney, Cambridge, 1936, p. 401). This would seem to provide the special and peculiar circumstances under which More might have occasion to see Warham every day without always speaking to him. As one of several counsel in a case being pleaded in Star Chamber before Warham as judge, More might well see the Chancellor without exchanging words with him. More's connection with the Royal Court at that time does not likely come to more than the kind of connection that a lawyer has with the judges before whom he regularly pleads. It has nothing to do with the favor or the service of the Crown, and More considered the two kinds of connection mutually exclusive. See Appendix B.

Appendix B

MORE AS UNDER SHERIFF

I have been able to find no satisfactory account of the duties of the Under Sheriff in the sixteenth century. Erasmus' scanty account of More's duties and perquisites in his letter to Hutten (N 3:395-396; A 4:999, lines 205-213) and More's explanation of his reluctance to resign the office (see above, Part Two, section 6) suggest the brief description in the text. Although Erasmus would ordinarily be a poor source for the details of London government practice, his description of More's work as Under Sheriff has a special claim to credence since it may have been examined by More himself. (This is suggested by P. W. Allen [4:999, line 211, n.] on the basis of a change in the remuneration imputed to the office in the 1529 printing of the letter.) There can be no doubt, in view of More's own statement, that it was as Under Sheriff of London that he represented the City's interests in litigation before the Royal Courts. The mechanics of this representation is perhaps indicated in the P. R. O. lists of proceedings in Chancery, Star Chamber, etc., where in many instances it is the sheriffs rather than the Lord Mayor and Aldermen who are party to the suit. Whether for this work the Under Sheriff received payment beyond the fees due him for acting as judge in the Sheriff's court is not clear. More's own predecessor as Under Sheriff succeeded to the Recordership. Harpsfield, pp. 312-313.

Epilogue to the Torchbook Edition

A PALINODE

Confession is good for the soul, and confession of error by a scholar is good for that advancement of learning to which theoretically he and all other scholars are committed. Moreover if he does not have to indulge in it too often, such confession only slightly detracts from his reputation for learning, while quite unwarrantedly it much enhances his reputation for magnanimity. This is especially so when he is lucky enough to be the first to point out his own errors before anyone else has publicly put the finger on them and him. And all these advantages are more than doubled when he can say, "I have erred on this and this point" (giving with one hand), "but it does not affect my central argument" (taking away with the other).

In this matter I am singularly blessed. In the introduction to *Utopia* in the Yale Edition of *The Works of St. Thomas More,* I have been able to do at considerable length all the things mentioned above, while here in the Torchbook reissue of *More's UTOPIA: The Biography of an Idea,* I can perform my penance more briefly at the very scene of my sins. (Hereafter to avoid confusion in titles the latter study will be referred to as *The Biography of an Idea.*)

As the reader of this book will have discovered by now, the reconstruction of More's idea for *Utopia* is here based on a very close and careful examination of the text of *Utopia* and of the correspondence which it evoked. The argument of *The Biography of an Idea* aimed to do four things:

1. To establish the *sequence* of writing of the sections of *Utopia.*
2. To establish the *place* of writing of the sections of *Utopia.*
3. To establish the *time* of writing of the sections of *Utopia.*
4. To establish the *foci of More's concern* when he wrote the two main sections of *Utopia.*

The crucial conclusions were that More wrote almost the whole of the second part before he wrote the first part;[1] that he wrote that second part in the Netherlands somewhere between the time of his arrival there in May and his departure in October, 1515;[2] that his

[1] *Biography of an Idea,* pp. 26-30.

focus of concern then was the *optimus status reipublicae,* the best ordering of a community;[3] that he wrote most of the first part in England probably in August, 1516;[4] and that his focus was then on the problem of counsel.[5] The bases of the argument on sequence, place, and focus were the paired references,[6] the tergiversations of what I have called "the curious paragraph,"[7] the veiled implications in More's letter of presentation to Giles,[8] Erasmus's assertion about the sequence of composition in his letter to Hutten,[9] and the sheer face value of the differences in substance, form, and tone between the Discourse on Utopia and the Dialogue of Counsel. Whatever solidity these bases originally possessed they have retained in the face of careful re-examination.

Although the evidence on sequence, place and focus withstands scrutiny, the evidence on precise time does not. More had certainly written some, probably most, of the Dialogue of Counsel before August, 1516. The argument to support the conjecture that More wrote it during Erasmus's stay with him in August involves the misinterpretation of the force of the adjective *nostram* in the phrase *Nusquamam nostram.*[10] A re-examination of More's correspondence indicates unfortunately that he did in fact sometimes use the first person singular nominative pronoun *ego* and relate it, still referring to himself alone, to some form of the first person plural *noster* or *nos.* Indeed referring to *Utopia* itself in a letter to Antonio (Bonvisi?), More writes of his surprise that *"Utopia nostra"* pleased Antonio so much since "I *(ego)* think [it] clearly deserves to hide itself away forever." So much for that argument. It is simply and patently worthless.

Moreover internal evidence in the Dialogue of Counsel makes the dating of part of that Dialogue as late as August quite impossible. Overlooked when *The Biography of an Idea* was written were two remarks in the text of the Dialogue that place a distinct chronological bracket around part of it. Two thirds of the way through, More writes of advisors of the king of France who tell him "by

[2] *Ibid.*
[3] *Ibid.,* p. 58, p. 81, p. 95.
[4] *Ibid.,* pp. 101-102.
[5] *Ibid.,* p. 102, p. 127.
[6] *Ibid.,* pp. 17-18.
[7] *Ibid.,* pp. 18-21.
[8] *Ibid.,* p. 28.
[9] N 3:398, A 4:999, lines 259-260.
[10] *Biography of an Idea,* pp. 99-102.

what crafty policies he may keep his hold on Milan," and who recommend that he make "a settlement . . . with the King of Aragon."[11] But Francis I could "keep his hold on Milan" only after he got hold of it by the battle of Marignano in mid-September, 1515; and he could make "a settlement . . . with the king of Aragon," Ferdinand, only prior to the latter's death on January 23, 1516. So More wrote this part of the Dialogue no earlier than mid-September, 1515 and not later than mid-February, 1516, when news of Ferdinand's death reached England.[12]

This correction as to time, it should be noted, does not diminish the likelihood that Erasmus knew whereof he spoke when in his letter to Hutten he described the *sequence* and the *circumstances* of the composition of *Utopia.* He was certainly a guest in More's house less than a month before he received the manuscript of *Utopia* from his friend.[13] That at that time More told him about *Utopia* and how he came to write it, and that Erasmus read the book then is, *prima facie,* very likely. That the two friends even got as far then as making plans for publication seems most probable from More's covering letter of transmittal of the book and Erasmus's acknowledgment of its receipt. More writes, "I send you our Nowhere, which is nowhere well written, and have prefixed to it a letter to my Peter [Giles]. For the rest I have learned by experience there is no need of my exhorting you to give it your best attention."[14] And Erasmus replies, "Peter Giles . . . is wonderfully struck by your Nusquama. . . . Every care shall be taken about the Island [i.e., *Utopia*]."[15] If Erasmus had not already seen *Utopia* and talked it over with More, this would be an astonishly laconic exchange. The apologetics and expressions of coy modesty with which humanists ordinarily sent their works to their friends are extraordinarily

[11] *U.* L. pp. 81-84, Y. S. pp. 54-55.

[12] There was, of course, a king of Aragon, Ferdinand's successor Charles, after Ferdinand's death; but the remark quoted could not have referred to him since the very next sentence describes him as "the prince of Castile." For a more detailed conjectural reconstruction of the Dialogue—this time, hopefully, free of factual errors—see the introduction to *Utopia* in the Yale Edition of the Works of St. Thomas More.

[13] *Biography of an Idea,* pp. 101-102.

[14] N. 2:381; A. 2:461. *Selected Letters,* E. F. Rogers, ed., New Haven, 1961, p. 73. The English translation in *Selected Letters* substitutes "my" for "nostram."

[15] N. 2:461, A. 2:474.

abridged in More's letter,[16] the literary squeals of delight with which those friends customarily received such works are wholly lacking in Erasmus's. Besides More does not write anything about what he expects Erasmus to do with the manuscript, nor does Erasmus write More what he intends to do with it. Yet he sets directly about getting *Utopia* published. Under the circumstances it seems reasonable to infer that apologetics, expressions of modesty, squeals of literary delight, instructions from More to Erasmus, and exact statements of intent from Erasmus to More were all rendered equally unnecessary from September on because they had all been taken care of *viva voce* when, the month before, the two friends talked together about the little book, and More told Erasmus of the sequence and circumstances of its writing.

* * *

The following passage appears near the very beginning of *Utopia*:

> When after a number of meetings there were certain points on which we could not agree sufficiently, they [the representatives of Archduke Charles] bade farewell to us for some days and left for Brussels to seek an official pronouncement from their prince. Meanwhile I, as business led me, made my way to Antwerp. While I stayed there, among my other visitors . . . was Peter Giles. . . . His delightful society and charming discourse made me less conscious than before of the separation from my wife and children to whom I was exceedingly anxious to get back; *for I had been more than four months away.*[17]

In *The Biography of an Idea* I missed the italicized clause. That clause sorts ill both with Erasmus's remark about the second part of *Utopia* being written at leisure and with the hint in the preceding passage that More had gone to Antwerp shortly after the departure of the representatives of the Archduke from Bruges, where negotiations had begun. That departure took place on July 21, and thereafter it seems that More was indeed at leisure. But if we take the italicized phrase literally, at the very earliest it was mid-September before More visited Antwerp and met Giles. Since he was preparing to leave the Netherlands by October 21, this allows at most about five weeks for More to visit Antwerp and write the

[16] Compare Rogers, 31, lines 33-4, *Selected Letters,* p. 89, "To William Warham"; Rogers, 34, *Selected Letters,* p. 90, "To Antonio [? Bonuisi]"; Rogers, 28, *Selected Letters,* p. 82, "To Cuthbert Turnstall."

[17] *U.* L. 25, Y. S. 27.

second part of *Utopia*. Such a tight schedule does not fit very well with Erasmus's notion that that part was written at leisure. This is especially so, since during the same period More was writing his letter to Dorp in defence of Erasmus, a letter itself only a couple of thousand words shorter than the second part of *Utopia*.

The simple way out of this dilemma is not to take the inconvenient clause literally. After all More was not composing his introduction to Utopia on strict historical principles for the edification, four hundred years later, of historians with finicking tastes in matters of chronology. He was getting on with his story as quickly as he could. The conflict among our three bits of evidence vanishes if we assume that in *Utopia* on grounds of literary amenity More conflated two visits to Antwerp, one shortly after the breakoff of negotiations on July 21, the other sometime between mid-September and mid-October. Again the evidence relating to the problem of chronology here discussed is presented at greater length in the introduction to *Utopia* previously mentioned.

Index

SINCE references to More's *Utopia* occur on almost every page of the preceding study, under the headings "More, Thomas," and "Utopia" I have included mainly information on the biography of the man and the history of the book. More's ideas in *Utopia* are separately indexed under appropriate subject headings. For a list of the more important headings, see under "Utopia." I have tried to distinguish throughout the index between *Utopia* the book and Utopia the place. Naturally all the more unpleasant work in connection with making this index was done by my wife, to whom I am ever grateful.

INDEX

Revised June, 1965

harper torchbooks

HUMANITIES AND SOCIAL SCIENCES

American Studies: General

THOMAS C. COCHRAN: The Inner Revolution: *Essays on the Social Sciences in History* TB/1140

EDWARD S. CORWIN: American Constitutional History. *Essays edited by Alpheus T. Mason and Gerald Garvey* TB/1136

A. HUNTER DUPREE: Science in the Federal Government: *A History of Policies and Activities to 1940* TB/573

OSCAR HANDLIN, Ed.: This Was America: *As Recorded by European Travelers in the Eighteenth, Nineteenth and Twentieth Centuries. Illus.* TB/1119

MARCUS LEE HANSEN: The Atlantic Migration: 1607-1860. *Edited by Arthur M. Schlesinger; Introduction by Oscar Handlin* TB/1052

MARCUS LEE HANSEN: The Immigrant in American History. *Edited with a Foreword by Arthur M. Schlesinger* TB/1120

JOHN HIGHAM, Ed.: The Reconstruction of American History TB/1068

ROBERT H. JACKSON: The Supreme Court in the American System of Government TB/1106

JOHN F. KENNEDY: A Nation of Immigrants. *Illus. Revised and Enlarged. Introduction by Robert F. Kennedy* TB/1118

RALPH BARTON PERRY: Puritanism and Democracy TB/1138

ARNOLD ROSE: The Negro in America: *The Condensed Version of Gunnar Myrdal's* An American Dilemma TB/3048

MAURICE R. STEIN: The Eclipse of Community: *An Interpretation of American Studies* TB/1128

W. LLOYD WARNER and Associates: Democracy in Jonesville: *A Study in Quality and Inequality* || TB/1129

W. LLOYD WARNER: Social Class in America: *The Evaluation of Status* TB/1013

American Studies: Colonial

BERNARD BAILYN: The New England Merchants in the Seventeenth Century TB/1149

JOSEPH CHARLES: The Origins of the American Party System TB/1049

LAWRENCE HENRY GIPSON: The Coming of the Revolution: 1763-1775. † *Illus.* TB/3007

LEONARD W. LEVY: Freedom of Speech and Press in Early American History: *Legacy of Suppression* TB/1109

PERRY MILLER: Errand Into the Wilderness TB/1139

PERRY MILLER & T. H. JOHNSON, Eds.: The Puritans: *A Sourcebook of Their Writings* Vol. I TB/1093; Vol. II TB/1094

KENNETH B. MURDOCK: Literature and Theology in Colonial New England TB/99

WALLACE NOTESTEIN: The English People on the Eve of Colonization: 1603-1630. † *Illus.* TB/3006

LOUIS B. WRIGHT: The Cultural Life of the American Colonies: 1607-1763. † *Illus.* TB/3005

American Studies: From the Revolution to the Civil War

JOHN R. ALDEN: The American Revolution: 1775-1783. † *Illus.* TB/3011

RAY A. BILLINGTON: The Far Western Frontier: 1830-1860. † *Illus.* TB/3012

GEORGE DANGERFIELD: The Awakening of American Nationalism: 1815-1828. † *Illus.* TB/3061

CLEMENT EATON: The Freedom-of-Thought Struggle in the Old South. *Revised and Enlarged. Illus.* TB/1150

CLEMENT EATON: The Growth of Southern Civilization: 1790-1860. † *Illus.* TB/3040

LOUIS FILLER: The Crusade Against Slavery: 1830-1860. † *Illus.* TB/3029

DIXON RYAN FOX: The Decline of Aristocracy in the Politics of New York: 1801-1840. ‡ *Edited by Robert V. Remini* TB/3064

FRANCIS J. GRUND: Aristocracy in America: *Social Class in the Formative Years of the New Nation* TB/1001

ALEXANDER HAMILTON: The Reports of Alexander Hamilton. ‡ *Edited by Jacob E. Cooke* TB/3060

DANIEL R. HUNDLEY: Social Relations in Our Southern States. ‡ *Edited by William R. Taylor* TB/3058

THOMAS JEFFERSON: Notes on the State of Virginia. ‡ *Edited by Thomas P. Abernethy* TB/3052

BERNARD MAYO: Myths and Men: *Patrick Henry, George Washington, Thomas Jefferson* TB/1108

JOHN C. MILLER: Alexander Hamilton and the Growth of the New Nation TB/3057

RICHARD B. MORRIS, Ed.: The Era of the American Revolution TB/1180

R. B. NYE: The Cultural Life of the New Nation: 1776-1801. † *Illus.* TB/3026

GEORGE E. PROBST, Ed.: The Happy Republic: *A Reader in Tocqueville's America* TB/1060

† The New American Nation Series, edited by Henry Steele Commager and Richard B. Morris.
‡ American Perspectives series, edited by Bernard Wishy and William E. Leuchtenburg.
* The Rise of Modern Europe series, edited by William L. Langer.
|| Researches in the Social, Cultural, and Behavioral Sciences, edited by Benjamin Nelson.
§ The Library of Religion and Culture, edited by Benjamin Nelson.
Σ Harper Modern Science Series, edited by James R. Newman.
° Not for sale in Canada.

FRANK THISTLETHWAITE: America and the Atlantic Community: *Anglo-American Aspects, 1790-1850* TB/1107

A. F. TYLER: Freedom's Ferment: *Phases of American Social History from the Revolution to the Outbreak of the Civil War. 31 illus.* TB/1074

GLYNDON G. VAN DEUSEN: The Jacksonian Era: 1828-1848. † *Illus.* TB/3028

LOUIS B. WRIGHT: Culture on the Moving Frontier TB/1053

American Studies: Since the Civil War

RAY STANNARD BAKER: Following the Color Line: *American Negro Citizenship in Progressive Era.* ‡ *Illus. Edited by Dewey W. Grantham, Jr.* TB/3053

RANDOLPH S. BOURNE: War and the Intellectuals: *Collected Essays, 1915-1919.* ‡ *Edited by Carl Resek* TB/3043

A. RUSSELL BUCHANAN: The United States and World War II. † *Illus.* Vol. I TB/3044; Vol. II TB/3045

ABRAHAM CAHAN: The Rise of David Levinsky: *a documentary novel of social mobility in early twentieth century America. Intro. by John Higham* TB/1028

THOMAS C. COCHRAN: The American Business System: *A Historical Perspective, 1900-1955* TB/1080

THOMAS C. COCHRAN & WILLIAM MILLER: The Age of Enterprise: *A Social History of Industrial America* TB/1054

FOSTER RHEA DULLES: America's Rise to World Power: 1898-1954. † *Illus.* TB/3021

W. A. DUNNING: Essays on the Civil War and Reconstruction. *Introduction by David Donald* TB/1181

W. A. DUNNING: Reconstruction, Political and Economic: 1865-1877 TB/1073

HAROLD U. FAULKNER: Politics, Reform and Expansion: 1890-1900. † *Illus.* TB/3020

JOHN D. HICKS: Republican Ascendancy: 1921-1933. † *Illus.* TB/3041

ROBERT HUNTER: Poverty: *Social Conscience in the Progressive Era.* ‡ *Edited by Robert d'A. Jones* TB/3065

HELEN HUNT JACKSON: A Century of Dishonor: *The Early Crusade for Indian Reform.* ‡ *Edited by Andrew F. Rolle* TB/3063

ALBERT D. KIRWAN: Revolt of the Rednecks: *Mississippi Politics, 1876-1925* TB/1199

WILLIAM L. LANGER & S. EVERETT GLEASON: The Challenge to Isolation: *The World Crisis of 1937-1940 and American Foreign Policy* Vol. I TB/3054; Vol. II TB/3055

WILLIAM E. LEUCHTENBURG: Franklin D. Roosevelt and the New Deal: 1932-1940. † *Illus.* TB/3025

ARTHUR S. LINK: Woodrow Wilson and the Progressive Era: 1910-1917. † *Illus.* TB/3023

ROBERT GREEN MCCLOSKEY: American Conservatism in the Age of Enterprise: 1865-1910 TB/1137

GEORGE E. MOWRY: The Era of Theodore Roosevelt and the Birth of Modern America: 1900-1912. † *Illus.* TB/3022

WALTER RAUSCHENBUSCH: Christianity and the Social Crisis. ‡ *Edited by Robert D. Cross* TB/3059

CHARLES H. SHINN: Mining Camps: *A Study in American Frontier Government.* ‡ *Edited by Rodman W. Paul* TB/3062

TWELVE SOUTHERNERS: I'll Take My Stand: *The South and the Agrarian Tradition. Intro. by Louis D. Rubin, Jr.; Biographical Essays by Virginia Rock* TB/1072

WALTER E. WEYL: The New Democracy: *An Essay on Certain Political Tendencies in the United States.* ‡ *Edited by Charles B. Forcey* TB/3042

VERNON LANE WHARTON: The Negro in Mississippi: 1865-1890 TB/1178

Anthropology

JACQUES BARZUN: Race: *A Study in Superstition. Revised Edition* TB/1172

JOSEPH B. CASAGRANDE, Ed.: In the Company of Man: *Twenty Portraits of Anthropological Informants. Illus.* TB/3047

W. E. LE GROS CLARK: The Antecedents of Man: *An Introduction to the Evolution of the Primates.* ° *Illus.* TB/559

CORA DU BOIS: The People of Alor. *New Preface by the author. Illus.* Vol. I TB/1042; Vol. II TB/1043

RAYMOND FIRTH, Ed.: Man and Culture: *An Evaluation of the Work of Bronislaw Malinowski* || ° TB/1133

L. S. B. LEAKEY: Adam's Ancestors: *The Evolution of Man and His Culture. Illus.* TB/1019

ROBERT H. LOWIE: Primitive Society. *Introduction by Fred Eggan* TB/1056

SIR EDWARD TYLOR: The Origins of Culture. *Part I of "Primitive Culture."* § *Introduction by Paul Radin* TB/33

SIR EDWARD TYLOR: Religion in Primitive Culture. *Part II of "Primitive Culture."* § *Introduction by Paul Radin* TB/34

W. LLOYD WARNER: A Black Civilization: *A Study of an Australian Tribe.* || *Illus.* TB/3056

Art and Art History

WALTER LOWRIE: Art in the Early Church. *152 illus. Revised Edition* TB/124

EMILE MÂLE: The Gothic Image: *Religious Art in France of the Thirteenth Century.* § *190 illus.* TB/44

MILLARD MEISS: Painting in Florence and Siena after the Black Death: *The Arts, Religion and Society in the Mid-Fourteenth Century. 169 illus.* TB/1148

ERICH NEUMANN: The Archetypal World of Henry Moore. *107 illus.* TB/2020

DORA & ERWIN PANOFSKY: Pandora's Box: *The Changing Aspects of a Mythical Symbol. Revised Edition. Illus.* TB/2021

ERWIN PANOFSKY: Studies in Iconology: *Humanistic Themes in the Art of the Renaissance. 180 illustrations* TB/1077

ALEXANDRE PIANKOFF: The Shrines of Tut-Ankh-Amon. *Edited by N. Rambova. 117 illus.* TB/2011

JEAN SEZNEC: The Survival of the Pagan Gods: *The Mythological Tradition and Its Place in Renaissance Humanism and Art. 108 illustrations* TB/2004

OTTO VON SIMSON: The Gothic Cathedral: *Origins of Gothic Architecture and the Medieval Concept of Order. 58 illus.* TB/2018

HEINRICH ZIMMER: Myth and Symbols in Indian Art and Civilization. *70 illustrations* TB/2005

Business, Economics & Economic History

REINHARD BENDIX: Work and Authority in Industry: *Ideologies of Management in the Course of Industrialization* TB/3035

GILBERT BURCK & EDITORS OF FORTUNE: The Computer Age TB/1179

THOMAS C. COCHRAN: The American Business System: *A Historical Perspective, 1900-1955* TB/1080

THOMAS C. COCHRAN: The Inner Revolution: *Essays on the Social Sciences in History* TB/1140

THOMAS C. COCHRAN & WILLIAM MILLER: The Age of Enterprise: *A Social History of Industrial America* TB/1054

ROBERT DAHL & CHARLES E. LINDBLOM: Politics, Economics, and Welfare: *Planning and Politico-Economic Systems Resolved into Basic Social Processes* TB/3037

PETER F. DRUCKER: The New Society: *The Anatomy of Industrial Order* TB/1082

EDITORS OF FORTUNE: America in the Sixties: *The Economy and the Society* TB/1015

ROBERT L. HEILBRONER: The Great Ascent: *The Struggle for Economic Development in Our Time* TB/3030

ABBA P. LERNER: Everybody's Business: *Current Assumptions in Economics and Public Policy* TB/3051

ROBERT GREEN MCCLOSKEY: American Conservatism in the Age of Enterprise, 1865-1910 TB/1137

PAUL MANTOUX: The Industrial Revolution in the Eighteenth Century: *The Beginnings of the Modern Factory System in England* ° TB/1079

WILLIAM MILLER, Ed.: Men in Business: *Essays on the Historical Role of the Entrepreneur* TB/1081

PERRIN STRYKER: The Character of the Executive: *Eleven Studies in Managerial Qualities* TB/1041

PIERRE URI: Partnership for Progress: *A Program for Transatlantic Action* TB/3036

Contemporary Culture

JACQUES BARZUN: The House of Intellect TB/1051

JOHN U. NEF: Cultural Foundations of Industrial Civilization TB/1024

NATHAN M. PUSEY: The Age of the Scholar: *Observations on Education in a Troubled Decade* TB/1157

PAUL VALÉRY: The Outlook for Intelligence TB/2016

History: General

L. CARRINGTON GOODRICH: A Short History of the Chinese People. *Illus.* TB/3015

DAN N. JACOBS & HANS H. BAERWALD: *Chinese Communism: Selected Documents* TB/3031

BERNARD LEWIS: The Arabs in History TB/1029

SIR PERCY SYKES: A History of Exploration. ° *Introduction by John K. Wright* TB/1046

History: Ancient and Medieval

A. ANDREWES: The Greek Tyrants TB/1103

P. BOISSONNADE: Life and Work in Medieval Europe: *The Evolution of the Medieval Economy, the Fifth to the Fifteenth Centuries.* ° *Preface by Lynn White, Jr.* TB/1141

HELEN CAM: England before Elizabeth TB/1026

NORMAN COHN: The Pursuit of the Millennium: *Revolutionary Messianism in Medieval and Reformation Europe and its Bearing on Modern Leftist and Rightist Totalitarian Movements* TB/1037

G. G. COULTON: Medieval Village, Manor, and Monastery TB/1022

HEINRICH FICHTENAU: The Carolingian Empire: *The Age of Charlemagne* TB/1142

F. L. GANSHOF: Feudalism TB/1058

EDWARD GIBBON: The Triumph of Christendom in the Roman Empire *(Chaps. XV-XX of "Decline and Fall," J. B. Bury edition).* § *Illus.* TB/46

MICHAEL GRANT: Ancient History ° TB/1190

DENYS HAY: The Medieval Centuries ° TB/1192

J. M. HUSSEY: The Byzantine World TB/1057

SAMUEL NOAH KRAMER: Sumerian Mythology TB/1055

FERDINAND LOT: The End of the Ancient World and the Beginnings of the Middle Ages. *Introduction by Glanville Downey* TB/1044

G. MOLLATT: The Popes at Avignon: 1305-1378 TB/308

CHARLES PETIT-DUTAILLIS: The Feudal Monarchy in France and England: *From the Tenth to the Thirteenth Century* ° TB/1165

HENRI PIERENNE: Early Democracies in the Low Countries: *Urban Society and Political Conflict in the Middle Ages and the Renaissance. Introduction by John H. Mundy* TB/1110

STEVEN RUNCIMAN: A History of the Crusades. Volume I: *The First Crusade and the Foundation of the Kingdom of Jerusalem. Illus.* TB/1143

FERDINAND SCHEVILL: Siena: *The History of a Medieval Commune. Introduction by William M. Bowsky* TB/1164

HENRY OSBORN TAYLOR: The Classical Heritage of the Middle Ages. *Foreword and Biblio. by Kenneth M. Setton* TB/1117

F. VAN DER MEER: Augustine The Bishop: *Church and Society at the Dawn of the Middle Ages* TB/304

J. M. WALLACE-HADRILL: The Barbarian West: *The Early Middle Ages, A.D. 400-1000* TB/1061

History: Renaissance & Reformation

JACOB BURCKHARDT: The Civilization of the Renaissance in Italy. *Introduction by Benjamin Nelson and Charles Trinkaus. Illus.* Vol. I TB/40; Vol. II TB/41

ERNST CASSIRER: The Individual and the Cosmos in Renaissance Philosophy. *Translated with an Introduction by Mario Domandi* TB/1097

FEDERICO CHABOD: Machiavelli and the Renaissance TB/1193

EDWARD P. CHEYNEY: The Dawn of a New Era, 1250-1453. * *Illus.* TB/3002

R. TREVOR DAVIES: The Golden Century of Spain, 1501-1621 ° TB/1194

DESIDERIUS ERASMUS: Christian Humanism and the Reformation: *Selected Writings. Edited and translated by John C. Olin* TB/1166

WALLACE K. FERGUSON et al.: Facets of the Renaissance TB/1098

WALLACE K. FERGUSON et al.: The Renaissance: *Six Essays. Illus.* TB/1084

JOHN NEVILLE FIGGIS: The Divine Right of Kings. *Introduction by G. R. Elton* TB/1191

JOHN NEVILLE FIGGIS: Political Thought from Gerson to Grotius: 1414-1625: *Seven Studies. Introduction by Garrett Mattingly* TB/1032

MYRON P. GILMORE: The World of Humanism, 1453-1517.* *Illus.* TB/3003

FRANCESCO GUICCIARDINI: Maxims and Reflections of a Renaissance Statesman *(Ricordi). Trans. by Mario Domandi. Intro. by Nicolai Rubinstein* TB/1160

J. H. HEXTER: More's Utopia: *The Biography of an Idea* TB/1195

JOHAN HUIZINGA: Erasmus and the Age of Reformation. *Illus.* TB/19

ULRICH VON HUTTEN et al.: On the Eve of the Reformation: *"Letters of Obscure Men." Introduction by Hajo Holborn* TB/1124

PAUL O. KRISTELLER: Renaissance Thought: *The Classic, Scholastic, and Humanist Strains* TB/1048

PAUL O. KRISTELLER: Renaissance Thought II: *Papers on Humanism and the Arts* TB/1163

NICCOLÒ MACHIAVELLI: History of Florence and of the Affairs of Italy: *from the earliest times to the death of Lorenzo the Magnificent. Introduction by Felix Gilbert* TB/1027

ALFRED VON MARTIN: Sociology of the Renaissance. *Introduction by Wallace K. Ferguson* TB/1099

GARRETT MATTINGLY et al.: Renaissance Profiles. *Edited by J. H. Plumb* TB/1162

MILLARD MEISS: Painting in Florence and Siena after the Black Death: *The Arts, Religion and Society in the Mid-Fourteenth Century. 169 illus.* TB/1148

J. E. NEALE: The Age of Catherine de Medici ° TB/1085

ERWIN PANOFSKY: Studies in Iconology: *Humanistic Themes in the Art of the Renaissance. 180 illustrations* TB/1077

J. H. PARRY: The Establishment of the European Hegemony: 1415-1715: *Trade and Exploration in the Age of the Renaissance* TB/1045

J. H. PLUMB: The Italian Renaissance: *A Concise Survey of Its History and Culture* TB/1161

GORDON RUPP: Luther's Progress to the Diet of Worms ° TB/120

FERDINAND SCHEVILL: The Medici. *Illus.* TB/1010

FERDINAND SCHEVILL: Medieval and Renaissance Florence. *Illus.* Volume I: *Medieval Florence* TB/1090 Volume II: *The Coming of Humanism and the Age of the Medici* TB/1091

G. M. TREVELYAN: England in the Age of Wycliffe, 1368-1520 ° TB/1112

VESPASIANO: Renaissance Princes, Popes, and Prelates: *The Vespasiano Memoirs: Lives of Illustrious Men of the XVth Century. Introduction by Myron P. Gilmore* TB/1111

History: Modern European

FREDERICK B. ARTZ: Reaction and Revolution, 1815-1832. * *Illus.* TB/3034

MAX BELOFF: The Age of Absolutism, 1660-1815 TB/1062

ROBERT C. BINKLEY: Realism and Nationalism, 1852-1871. * *Illus.* TB/3038

CRANE BRINTON: A Decade of Revolution, 1789-1799. * *Illus.* TB/3018

J. BRONOWSKI & BRUCE MAZLISH: The Western Intellectual Tradition: *From Leonardo to Hegel* TB/3001

GEOFFREY BRUUN: Europe and the French Imperium, 1799-1814. * *Illus.* TB/3033

ALAN BULLOCK: Hitler, A Study in Tyranny. ° *Illus.* TB/1123

E. H. CARR: The Twenty Years' Crisis, 1919-1939: *An Introduction to the Study of International Relations* ° TB/1122

GORDON A. CRAIG: From Bismarck to Adenauer: *Aspects of German Statecraft. Revised Edition* TB/1171

WALTER L. DORN: Competition for Empire, 1740-1763. * *Illus.* TB/3032

CARL J. FRIEDRICH: The Age of the Baroque, 1610-1660. * *Illus.* TB/3004

RENÉ FUELOEP-MILLER: The Mind and Face of Bolshevism: *An Examination of Cultural Life in Soviet Russia. New Epilogue by the Author* TB/1188

M. DOROTHY GEORGE: London Life in the Eighteenth Century TB/1182

LEO GERSHOY: From Despotism to Revolution, 1763-1789. * *Illus.* TB/3017

C. C. GILLISPIE: Genesis and Geology: *The Decades before Darwin* § TB/51

ALBERT GOODWIN: The French Revolution TB/1064

ALBERT GUERARD: France in the Classical Age: *The Life and Death of an Ideal* TB/1183

CARLTON J. H. HAYES: A Generation of Materialism, 1871-1900. * *Illus.* TB/3039

J. H. HEXTER: Reappraisals in History: *New Views on History and Society in Early Modern Europe* TB/1100

A. R. HUMPHREYS: The Augustan World: *Society, Thought, and Letters in Eighteenth Century England* TB/1105

ALDOUS HUXLEY: The Devils of Loudun: *A Study in the Psychology of Power Politics and Mystical Religion in the France of Cardinal Richelieu* § ° TB/60

DAN N. JACOBS, Ed.: The New Communist Manifesto *and Related Documents. Third edition, revised* TB/1078

HANS KOHN, Ed.: The Mind of Modern Russia: *Historical and Political Thought of Russia's Great Age* TB/1065

KINGSLEY MARTIN: French Liberal Thought in the Eighteenth Century: *A Study of Political Ideas from Bayle to Condorcet* TB/1114

SIR LEWIS NAMIER: Personalities and Powers: *Selected Essays* TB/1186

SIR LEWIS NAMIER: Vanished Supremacies: *Essays on European History, 1812-1918* ° TB/1088

JOHN U. NEF: Western Civilization Since the Renaissance: *Peace, War, Industry, and the Arts* TB/1113

FREDERICK L. NUSSBAUM: The Triumph of Science and Reason, 1660-1685. * *Illus.* TB/3009

JOHN PLAMENATZ: German Marxism and Russian Communism. ° *New Preface by the Author* TB/1189

RAYMOND W. POSTGATE, Ed.: Revolution from 1789 to 1906: *Selected Documents* TB/1063

PENFIELD ROBERTS: The Quest for Security, 1715-1740. * *Illus.* TB/3016

PRISCILLA ROBERTSON: Revolutions of 1848: *A Social History* TB/1025

ALBERT SOREL: Europe Under the Old Regime. *Translated by Francis H. Herrick* TB/1121

N. N. SUKHANOV: The Russian Revolution, 1917: *Eyewitness Account. Edited by Joel Carmichael* Vol. I TB/1066; Vol. II TB/1067

A. J. P. TAYLOR: The Habsburg Monarch, 1809-1918: *A History of the Austrian Empire and Austria-Hungary* ° TB/1187

JOHN B. WOLF: The Emergence of the Great Powers, 1685-1715. * *Illus.* TB/3010

JOHN B. WOLF: France: 1814-1919: *The Rise of a Liberal-Democratic Society* TB/3019

Intellectual History

HERSCHEL BAKER: The Image of Man: *A Study of the Idea of Human Dignity in Classical Antiquity, the Middle Ages, and the Renaissance* TB/1047

R. R. BOLGAR: The Classical Heritage and Its Beneficiaries: *From the Carolingian Age to the End of the Renaissance* TB/1125

J. BRONOWSKI & BRUCE MAZLISH: The Western Intellectual Tradition: *From Leonardo to Hegel* TB/3001

ERNST CASSIRER: The Individual and the Cosmos in Renaissance Philosophy. *Translated with an Introduction by Mario Domandi* TB/1097

NORMAN COHN: The Pursuit of the Millennium: *Revolutionary Messianism in medieval and Reformation Europe and its bearing on modern Leftist and Rightist totalitarian movements* TB/1037

G. RACHEL LEVY: Religious Conceptions of the Stone Age and Their Influence upon European Thought. *Illus. Introduction by Henri Frankfort* TB/106

ARTHUR O. LOVEJOY: The Great Chain of Being: *A Study of the History of an Idea* TB/1009

MILTON C. NAHM: Genius and Creativity: *An Essay in the History of Ideas* TB/1196

ROBERT PAYNE: Hubris: *A Study of Pride. Foreword by Sir Herbert Read* TB/1031

RALPH BARTON PERRY: The Thought and Character of William James: *Briefer Version* TB/1156

BRUNO SNELL: The Discovery of the Mind: *The Greek Origins of European Thought* TB/1018

ERNEST LEE TUVESON: Millennium and Utopia: *A Study in the Background of the Idea of Progress.* ‖ *New Preface by the Author* TB/1134

PAUL VALÉRY: The Outlook for Intelligence TB/2016

Literature, Poetry, The Novel & Criticism

JAMES BAIRD: Ishmael: *The Art of Melville in the Contexts of International Primitivism* TB/1023

JACQUES BARZUN: The House of Intellect TB/1051

W. J. BATE: From Classic to Romantic: *Premises of Taste in Eighteenth Century England* TB/1036

RACHEL BESPALOFF: On the Iliad TB/2006

R. P. BLACKMUR et al.: Lectures in Criticism. *Introduction by Huntington Cairns* TB/2003

RANDOLPH S. BOURNE: War and the Intellectuals: *Collected Essays, 1915-1919.* ‡ *Edited by Carl Resek* TB/3043

ABRAHAM CAHAN: The Rise of David Levinsky: *a documentary novel of social mobility in early twentieth century America. Introduction by John Higham* TB/1028

ERNST R. CURTIUS: European Literature and the Latin Middle Ages TB/2015

GEORGE ELIOT: Daniel Deronda: *a novel. Introduction by F. R. Leavis* TB/1039

ETIENNE GILSON: Dante and Philosophy TB/1089

ALFRED HARBAGE: As They Liked It: *A Study of Shakespeare's Moral Artistry* TB/1035

STANLEY R. HOPPER, Ed.: Spiritual Problems in Contemporary Literature § TB/21

A. R. HUMPHREYS: The Augustan World: *Society, Thought and Letters in Eighteenth Century England* ° TB/1105

ALDOUS HUXLEY: Antic Hay & The Giaconda Smile. ° *Introduction by Martin Green* TB/3503

ALDOUS HUXLEY: Brave New World & Brave New World Revisited. ° *Introduction by Martin Green* TB/3501

HENRY JAMES: Roderick Hudson: *a novel. Introduction by Leon Edel* TB/1016

HENRY JAMES: The Tragic Muse: *a novel. Introduction by Leon Edel* TB/1017

ARNOLD KETTLE: An Introduction to the English Novel.
Volume I: *Defoe to George Eliot* TB/1011
Volume II: *Henry James to the Present* TB/1012

ROGER SHERMAN LOOMIS: The Development of Arthurian Romance TB/1167

JOHN STUART MILL: On Bentham and Coleridge. *Introduction by F. R. Leavis* TB/1070

PERRY MILLER & T. H. JOHNSON, Editors: The Puritans: *A Sourcebook of Their Writings* Vol. I TB/1093; Vol. II TB/1094

KENNETH B. MURDOCK: Literature and Theology in Colonial New England TB/99

SAMUEL PEPYS: The Diary of Samuel Pepys. ° *Edited by O. F. Morshead. Illus. by Ernest Shepard* TB/1007

ST.-JOHN PERSE: Seamarks TB/2002

O. E. RÖLVAAG: Giants in the Earth TB/3504

GEORGE SANTAYANA: Interpretations of Poetry and Religion § TB/9

C. P. SNOW: Time of Hope: *a novel* TB/1040

HEINRICH STRAUMANN: American Literature in the Twentieth Century. *Third Edition, Revised* TB/1168

DOROTHY VAN GHENT: The English Novel: *Form and Function* TB/1050

E. B. WHITE: One Man's Meat. *Introduction by Walter Blair* TB/3505

MORTON DAUWEN ZABEL, Editor: Literary Opinion in America Vol. I TB/3013; Vol. II TB/3014

Myth, Symbol & Folklore

JOSEPH CAMPBELL, Editor: Pagan and Christian Mysteries *Illus.* TB/2013

MIRCEA ELIADE: Cosmos and History: *The Myth of the Eternal Return* § TB/2050

C. G. JUNG & C. KERÉNYI: Essays on a Science of Mythology: *The Myths of the Divine Child and the Divine Maiden* TB/2014

DORA & ERWIN PANOFSKY: Pandora's Box: *The Changing Aspects of a Mythical Symbol. Revised Edition. Illus.* TB/2021

ERWIN PANOFSKY: Studies in Iconology: *Humanistic Themes in the Art of the Renaissance. 180 illustrations* TB/1077

JEAN SEZNEC: The Survival of the Pagan Gods: *The Mythological Tradition and its Place in Renaissance Humanism and Art. 108 illustrations* TB/2004

HELLMUT WILHELM: Change: *Eight Lectures on the I Ching* TB/2019

HEINRICH ZIMMER: Myths and Symbols in Indian Art and Civilization. *70 illustrations* TB/2005

Philosophy

HENRI BERGSON: Time and Free Will: *An Essay on the Immediate Data of Consciousness* ° TB/1021

H. J. BLACKHAM: Six Existentialist Thinkers: *Kierkegaard, Nietzsche, Jaspers, Marcel, Heidegger, Sartre* ° TB/1002

CRANE BRINTON: Nietzsche. *New Preface and Epilogue by the Author* TB/1197

ERNST CASSIRER: The Individual and the Cosmos in Renaissance Philosophy. *Translated with an Introduction by Mario Domandi* TB/1097

ERNST CASSIRER: Rousseau, Kant and Goethe. *Introduction by Peter Gay* TB/1092

FREDERICK COPLESTON: Medieval Philosophy ° TB/376

F. M. CORNFORD: From Religion to Philosophy: *A Study in the Origins of Western Speculation* § TB/20

WILFRID DESAN: The Tragic Finale: *An Essay on the Philosophy of Jean-Paul Sartre* TB/1030

PAUL FRIEDLÄNDER: Plato: *An Introduction* TB/2017

ÉTIENNE GILSON: Dante and Philosophy TB/1089

WILLIAM CHASE GREENE: Moira: *Fate, Good, and Evil in Greek Thought* TB/1104

W. K. C. GUTHRIE: The Greek Philosophers: *From Thales to Aristotle* ° TB/1008

F. H. HEINEMANN: Existentialism and the Modern Predicament TB/28

EDMUND HUSSERL: Phenomenology and the Crisis of Philosophy. *Translated with an Introduction by Quentin Lauer* TB/1170

IMMANUEL KANT: The Doctrine of Virtue, *being Part II of The Metaphysic of Morals. Translated with Notes and Introduction by Mary J. Gregor. Foreword by H. J. Paton* TB/110

IMMANUEL KANT: Groundwork of the Metaphysic of Morals. *Translated and analyzed by H. J. Paton* TB/1159

IMMANUEL KANT: Lectures on Ethics. § *Introduction by Lewis W. Beck* TB/105

QUENTIN LAUER: Phenomenology: *Its Genesis and Prospect* TB/1169

GEORGE A. MORGAN: What Nietzsche Means TB/1198

MICHAEL POLANYI: Personal Knowledge: *Towards a Post-Critical Philosophy* TB/1158

WILLARD VAN ORMAN QUINE: Elementary Logic. *Revised Edition* TB/577

WILLARD VAN ORMAN QUINE: From a Logical Point of View: *Logico-Philosophical Essays* TB/566

BERTRAND RUSSELL et al.: The Philosophy of Bertrand Russell. *Edited by Paul Arthur Schilpp*
Vol. I TB/1095; Vol. II TB/1096

L. S. STEBBING: A Modern Introduction to Logic TB/538

ALFRED NORTH WHITEHEAD: Process and Reality: *An Essay in Cosmology* TB/1033

WILHELM WINDELBAND: A History of Philosophy
Vol. I: *Greek, Roman, Medieval* TB/38
Vol. II: *Renaissance, Enlightenment, Modern* TB/39

Philosophy of History

NICOLAS BERDYAEV: The Beginning and the End § TB/14

NICOLAS BERDYAEV: The Destiny of Man TB/61

WILHELM DILTHEY: Pattern and Meaning in History: *Thoughts on History and Society.* ° *Edited with an Introduction by H. P. Rickman* TB/1075

RAYMOND KLIBANSKY & H. J. PATON, Eds.: Philosophy and History: *The Ernst Cassirer Festschrift. Illus.* TB/1115

MILTON C. NAHM: Genius and Creativity: *An Essay in the History of Ideas* TB/1196

JOSE ORTEGA Y GASSET: The Modern Theme. *Introduction by Jose Ferrater Mora* TB/1038

KARL R. POPPER: The Poverty of Historicism ° TB/1126

W. H. WALSH: Philosophy of History: *An Introduction* TB/1020

Political Science & Government

JEREMY BENTHAM: The Handbook of Political Fallacies: *Introduction by Crane Brinton* TB/1069

KENNETH E. BOULDING: Conflict and Defense: *A General Theory* TB/3024

CRANE BRINTON: English Political Thought in the Nineteenth Century TB/1071

EDWARD S. CORWIN: American Constitutional History: *Essays edited by Alpheus T. Mason and Gerald Garvey* TB/1136

ROBERT DAHL & CHARLES E. LINDBLOM: Politics, Economics, and Welfare: *Planning and Politico-Economic Systems Resolved into Basic Social Processes* TB/3037

JOHN NEVILLE FIGGIS: The Divine Right of Kings. *Introduction by G. R. Elton* TB/1191

JOHN NEVILLE FIGGIS: Political Thought from Gerson to Grotius: 1414-1625: *Seven Studies. Introduction by Garrett Mattingly* TB/1032

F. L. GANSHOF: Feudalism TB/1058

G. P. GOOCH: English Democratic Ideas in Seventeenth Century TB/1006

J. H. HEXTER: More's Utopia: *The Biography of an Idea. New Epilogue by the Author* TB/1195

ROBERT H. JACKSON: The Supreme Court in the American System of Government TB/1106

DAN N. JACOBS, Ed.: The New Communist Manifesto *and Related Documents* TB/1078

DAN N. JACOBS & HANS BAERWALD, Eds.: Chinese Communism: *Selected Documents* TB/3031

ROBERT GREEN MCCLOSKEY: American Conservatism in the Age of Enterprise, 1865-1910 TB/1137

KINGSLEY MARTIN: French Liberal Thought in the Eighteenth Century: *Political Ideas from Bayle to Condorcet* TB/1114

JOHN STUART MILL: On Bentham and Coleridge. *Introduction by F. R. Leavis* TB/1070

JOHN B. MORRALL: Political Thought in Medieval Times TB/1076

JOHN PLAMENATZ: German Marxism and Russian Communism. ° *New Preface by the Author* TB/1189

KARL R. POPPER: The Open Society and Its Enemies
Vol. I: *The Spell of Plato* TB/1101
Vol. II: *The High Tide of Prophecy: Hegel, Marx, and the Aftermath* TB/1102

HENRI DE SAINT-SIMON: Social Organization, The Science of Man, and Other Writings. *Edited and Translated by Felix Markham* TB/1152

JOSEPH A. SCHUMPETER: Capitalism, Socialism and Democracy TB/3008

CHARLES H. SHINN: Mining Camps: *A Study in American Frontier Government.* ‡ *Edited by Rodman W. Paul* TB/3062

Psychology

ALFRED ADLER: The Individual Psychology of Alfred Adler. *Edited by Heinz L. and Rowena R. Ansbacher* TB/1154

ALFRED ADLER: Problems of Neurosis. *Introduction by Heinz L. Ansbacher* TB/1145

ANTON T. BOISEN: The Exploration of the Inner World: *A Study of Mental Disorder and Religious Experience* TB/87

HERBERT FINGARETTE: The Self in Transformation: *Psychoanalysis, Philosophy and the Life of the Spirit.* || TB/1177

SIGMUND FREUD: On Creativity and the Unconscious: *Papers on the Psychology of Art, Literature, Love, Religion.* § *Intro. by Benjamin Nelson* TB/45

C. JUDSON HERRICK: The Evolution of Human Nature TB/545

WILLIAM JAMES: Psychology: *The Briefer Course. Edited with an Intro. by Gordon Allport* TB/1034

C. G. JUNG: Psychological Reflections TB/2001

C. G. JUNG: Symbols of Transformation: *An Analysis of the Prelude to a Case of Schizophrenia. Illus.*
Vol. I: TB/2009; Vol. II TB/2010

C. G. JUNG & C. KERÉNYI: Essays on a Science of Mythology: *The Myths of the Divine Child and the Divine Maiden* TB/2014

JOHN T. MCNEILL: A History of the Cure of Souls TB/126

KARL MENNINGER: Theory of Psychoanalytic Technique TB/1144

ERICH NEUMANN: Amor and Psyche: *The Psychic Development of the Feminine* TB/2012

ERICH NEUMANN: The Archetypal World of Henry Moore. *107 illus.* TB/2020

ERICH NEUMANN: The Origins and History of Consciousness Vol. I *Illus.* TB/2007; Vol. II TB/2008

C. P. OBERNDORF: A History of Psychoanalysis in America TB/1147

RALPH BARTON PERRY: The Thought and Character of William James: *Briefer Version* TB/1156

JEAN PIAGET, BÄRBEL INHELDER, & ALINA SZEMINSKA: The Child's Conception of Geometry ° TB/1146

JOHN H. SCHAAR: Escape from Authority: *The Perspectives of Erich Fromm* TB/1155

Sociology

JACQUES BARZUN: Race: *A Study in Superstition. Revised Edition* TB/1172

BERNARD BERELSON, Ed.: The Behavioral Sciences Today TB/1127

ABRAHAM CAHAN: The Rise of David Levinsky: *A documentary novel of social mobility in early twentieth century America. Intro. by John Higham* TB/1028

THOMAS C. COCHRAN: The Inner Revolution: *Essays on the Social Sciences in History* TB/1140

ALLISON DAVIS & JOHN DOLLARD: Children of Bondage: *The Personality Development of Negro Youth in the Urban South* || TB/3049

ST. CLAIR DRAKE & HORACE R. CAYTON: Black Metropolis: *A Study of Negro Life in a Northern City. Revised and Enlarged. Intro. by Everett C. Hughes* Vol. I TB/1086; Vol. II TB/1087

EMILE DURKHEIM et al.: Essays on Sociology and Philosophy: *With Analyses of Durkheim's Life and Work.* || *Edited by Kurt H. Wolff* TB/1151

LEON FESTINGER, HENRY W. RIECKEN & STANLEY SCHACHTER: When Prophecy Fails: *A Social and Psychological Account of a Modern Group that Predicted the Destruction of the World* || TB/1132

ALVIN W. GOULDNER: Wildcat Strike: *A Study in Worker-Management Relationships* || TB/1176

FRANCIS J. GRUND: Aristocracy in America: *Social Class in the Formative Years of the New Nation* TB/1001

KURT LEWIN: Field Theory in Social Science: *Selected Theoretical Papers.* || *Edited with a Foreword by* Dorwin Cartwright TB/1135

R. M. MACIVER: Social Causation TB/1153

ROBERT K. MERTON, LEONARD BROOM, LEONARD S. COTTRELL, JR., Editors: Sociology Today: *Problems and Prospects* || Vol. I TB/1173; Vol. II TB/1174

TALCOTT PARSONS & EDWARD A. SHILS, Editors: Toward a General Theory of Action: *Theoretical Foundations for the Social Sciences* TB/1083

JOHN H. ROHRER & MUNRO S. EDMONSON, Eds.: The Eighth Generation Grows Up: *Cultures and Personalities of New Orleans Negroes* || TB/3050

ARNOLD ROSE: The Negro in America: *The Condensed Version of Gunnar Myrdal's* An American Dilemma TB/3048

KURT SAMUELSSON: Religion and Economic Action: *A Critique of Max Weber's* The Protestant Ethic and the Spirit of Capitalism. || ° *Trans. by E. G. French; Ed. with Intro. by D. C. Coleman* TB/1131

PITIRIM A. SOROKIN: Contemporary Sociological Theories. *Through the First Quarter of the 20th Century* TB/3046

MAURICE R. STEIN: The Eclipse of Community: *An Interpretation of American Studies* TB/1128

FERDINAND TÖNNIES: Community and Society: *Gemeinschaft und Gesellschaft. Translated and edited by Charles P. Loomis* TB/1116

W. LLOYD WARNER & Associates: Democracy in Jonesville: *A Study in Quality and Inequality* TB/1129

W. LLOYD WARNER: Social Class in America: *The Evaluation of Status* TB/1013

RELIGION

Ancient & Classical

J. H. BREASTED: Development of Religion and Thought in Ancient Egypt. *Introduction by John A. Wilson* TB/57

HENRI FRANKFORT: Ancient Egyptian Religion: *An Interpretation* TB/77

G. RACHEL LEVY: Religious Conceptions of the Stone Age *and their Influence upon European Thought. Illus. Introduction by Henri Frankfort* TB/106

MARTIN P. NILSSON: Greek Folk Religion. *Foreword by Arthur Darby Nock* TB/78

ALEXANDRE PIANKOFF: The Shrines of Tut-Ankh-Amon. *Edited by N. Rambova. 117 illus.* TB/2011

H. J. ROSE: Religion in Greece and Rome TB/55

Biblical Thought & Literature

W. F. ALBRIGHT: The Biblical Period from Abraham to Ezra TB/102

C. K. BARRETT, Ed.: The New Testament Background: *Selected Documents* TB/86

C. H. DODD: The Authority of the Bible TB/43

M. S. ENSLIN: Christian Beginnings TB/5

M. S. ENSLIN: The Literature of the Christian Movement TB/6

JOHN GRAY: Archaeology and the Old Testament World. *Illus.* TB/127

H. H. ROWLEY: The Growth of the Old Testament TB/107

D. WINTON THOMAS, Ed.: Documents from Old Testament Times TB/85

The Judaic Tradition

MARTIN BUBER: Eclipse of God: *Studies in the Relation Between Religion and Philosophy* TB/12

MARTIN BUBER: Moses: *The Revelation and the Covenant* TB/27

MARTIN BUBER: Pointing the Way. *Introduction by Maurice S. Friedman* TB/103

MARTIN BUBER: The Prophetic Faith TB/73

MARTIN BUBER: Two Types of Faith: *the interpenetration of Judaism and Christianity* ° TB/75

ERNST LUDWIG EHRLICH: A Concise History of Israel: *From the Earliest Times to the Destruction of the Temple in A.D. 70* ° TB/128

MAURICE S. FRIEDMAN: Martin Buber: *The Life of Dialogue* TB/64

FLAVIUS JOSEPHUS: The Great Roman-Jewish War, *with* The Life of Josephus. *Introduction by William R. Farmer* TB/74

T. J. MEEK: Hebrew Origins TB/69

Christianity: Origins & Early Development

AUGUSTINE: An Augustine Synthesis. *Edited by Erich Przywara* TB/335

ADOLF DEISSMANN: Paul: *A Study in Social and Religious History* TB/15

EDWARD GIBBON: The Triumph of Christendom in the Roman Empire *(Chaps. XV-XX of "Decline and Fall," J. B. Bury edition).* § *Illus.* TB/46

MAURICE GOGUEL: Jesus and the Origins of Christianity. ° *Introduction by C. Leslie Mitton*
Volume I: *Prolegomena to the Life of Jesus* TB/65
Volume II: *The Life of Jesus* TB/66

EDGAR J. GOODSPEED: A Life of Jesus TB/1

ADOLF HARNACK: The Mission and Expansion of Christianity *in the First Three Centuries. Introduction by Jaroslav Pelikan* TB/92

R. K. HARRISON: The Dead Sea Scrolls: *An Introduction* ° TB/84

EDWIN HATCH: The Influence of Greek Ideas on Christianity. § *Introduction and Bibliography by Frederick C. Grant* TB/18

ARTHUR DARBY NOCK: Early Gentile Christianity and Its Hellenistic Background TB/111

ARTHUR DARBY NOCK: St. Paul ° TB/104

F. VAN DER MEER: Augustine the Bishop: *Church and Society at the Dawn of the Middle Ages* TB/304

JOHANNES WEISS: Earliest Christianity: *A History of the Period A.D. 30-150. Introduction and Bibliography by Frederick C. Grant* Volume I TB/53
Volume II TB/54

Christianity: The Middle Ages and The Reformation

JOHANNES ECKHART: Meister Eckhart: *A Modern Translation by R. B. Blakney* TB/8

DESIDERIUS ERASMUS: Christian Humanism and the Reformation: *Selected Writings. Edited and translated by John C. Olin* TB/1166

ÉTIENNE GILSON: Dante and Philosophy TB/1089

WILLIAM HALLER: The Rise of Puritanism TB/22

JOHAN HUIZINGA: Erasmus and the Age of Reformation. *Illus.* TB/19

A. C. MCGIFFERT: Protestant Thought Before Kant. *Preface by Jaroslav Pelikan* TB/93

JOHN T. MCNEILL: Makers of the Christian Tradition: *From Alfred the Great to Schleiermacher* TB/121

G. MOLLAT: The Popes at Avignon, 1305-1378 TB/308

GORDON RUPP: Luther's Progress to the Diet of Worms ° TB/120

Christianity: The Protestant Tradition

KARL BARTH: Church Dogmatics: *A Selection* TB/95

KARL BARTH: Dogmatics in Outline TB/56

KARL BARTH: The Word of God and the Word of Man TB/13

WINTHROP HUDSON: The Great Tradition of the American Churches TB/98

SOREN KIERKEGAARD: Edifying Discourses. *Edited with an Introduction by Paul Holmer* TB/32

SOREN KIERKEGAARD: The Journals of Kierkegaard. ° *Edited with an Introduction by Alexander Dru* TB/52

SOREN KIERKEGAARD: The Point of View for My Work as an Author: *A Report to History.* § *Preface by Benjamin Nelson* TB/88

SOREN KIERKEGAARD: The Present Age. § *Translated and edited by Alexander Dru. Introduction by Walter Kaufmann* TB/94

SOREN KIERKEGAARD: Purity of Heart TB/4

SOREN KIERKEGAARD: Repetition: *An Essay in Experimental Psychology. Translated with Introduction & Notes by Walter Lowrie* TB/117

SOREN KIERKEGAARD: Works of Love: *Some Christian Reflections in the Form of Discourses* TB/122

WALTER LOWRIE: Kierkegaard: *A Life* Vol. I TB/89
Vol. II TB/90

PERRY MILLER & T. H. JOHNSON, Editors: The Puritans: *A Sourcebook of Their Writings* Vol. I TB/1093
Vol. II TB/1094

F. SCHLEIERMACHER: The Christian Faith. *Introduction by Richard R. Niebuhr* Vol. I TB/108
Vol. II TB/109

F. SCHLEIERMACHER: On Religion: *Speeches to Its Cultured Despisers. Intro. by Rudolf Otto* TB/36

PAUL TILLICH: Dynamics of Faith TB/42

EVELYN UNDERHILL: Worship TB/10

G. VAN DER LEEUW: Religion in Essence and Manifestation: *A Study in Phenomenology. Appendices by Hans H. Penner* Vol. I TB/100; Vol. II TB/101

Christianity: The Roman and Eastern Traditions

A. ROBERT CAPONIGRI, Ed.: Modern Catholic Thinkers I: *God and Man* TB/306

A. ROBERT CAPONIGRI, Ed.: Modern Catholic Thinkers II: *The Church and the Political Order* TB/307

THOMAS CORBISHLEY, S. J.: Roman Catholicism TB/112

CHRISTOPHER DAWSON: The Historic Reality of Christian Culture TB/305

G. P. FEDOTOV: The Russian Religious Mind: *Kievan Christianity, the tenth to the thirteenth centuries* TB/70

G. P. FEDOTOV, Ed.: A Treasury of Russian Spirituality TB/303

DAVID KNOWLES: The English Mystical Tradition TB/302

GABRIEL MARCEL: Homo Viator: *Introduction to a Metaphysic of Hope* TB/397

GUSTAVE WEIGEL, S. J.: Catholic Theology in Dialogue TB/301

Oriental Religions: Far Eastern, Near Eastern

TOR ANDRAE: Mohammed: *The Man and His Faith* TB/62

EDWARD CONZE: Buddhism: *Its Essence and Development.* ° *Foreword by Arthur Waley* TB/58

EDWARD CONZE et al., Editors: Buddhist Texts Through the Ages TB/113

ANANDA COOMARASWAMY: Buddha and the Gospel of Buddhism. *Illus.* TB/119

H. G. CREEL: Confucius and the Chinese Way TB/63

FRANKLIN EDGERTON, Trans. & Ed.: The Bhagavad Gita TB/115

SWAMI NIKHILANANDA, Trans. & Ed.: The Upanishads: *A One-Volume Abridgment* TB/114

HELLMUT WILHELM: Change: *Eight Lectures on the I Ching* TB/2019

Philosophy of Religion

RUDOLF BULTMANN: History and Eschatology: *The Presence of Eternity* ° TB/91

RUDOLF BULTMANN AND FIVE CRITICS: Kerygma and Myth: *A Theological Debate* TB/80

RUDOLF BULTMANN and KARL KUNDSIN: Form Criticism: *Two Essays on New Testament Research. Translated by Frederick C. Grant* TB/96

MIRCEA ELIADE: The Sacred and the Profane TB/81

LUDWIG FEUERBACH: The Essence of Christianity. § *Introduction by Karl Barth. Foreword by H. Richard Niebuhr* TB/11

ADOLF HARNACK: What is Christianity? § *Introduction by Rudolf Bultmann* TB/17

FRIEDRICH HEGEL: On Christianity: *Early Theological Writings. Edited by Richard Kroner and T. M. Knox* TB/79

KARL HEIM: Christian Faith and Natural Science TB/16

IMMANUEL KANT: Religion Within the Limits of Reason Alone. § *Introduction by Theodore M. Greene and John Silber* TB/67

JOHN MACQUARRIE: An Existentialist Theology: *A Comparison of Heidegger and Bultmann.* ° *Preface by Rudolf Bultmann* TB/125

PAUL RAMSEY, Ed.: Faith and Ethics: *The Theology of H. Richard Niebuhr* TB/129

PIERRE TEILHARD DE CHARDIN: The Phenomenon of Man ° TB/83

Religion, Culture & Society

JOSEPH L. BLAU, Ed.: Cornerstones of Religious Freedom in America: *Selected Basic Documents, Court Decisions and Public Statements. Revised and Enlarged Edition* TB/118

C. C. GILLISPIE: Genesis and Geology: *The Decades before Darwin* § TB/51

KYLE HASELDEN: The Racial Problem in Christian Perspective TB/116

WALTER KAUFMANN, Ed.: Religion from Tolstoy to Camus: *Basic Writings on Religious Truth and Morals. Enlarged Edition* TB/123

JOHN T. MCNEILL: A History of the Cure of Souls TB/126

KENNETH B. MURDOCK: Literature and Theology in Colonial New England TB/99

H. RICHARD NIEBUHR: Christ and Culture TB/3

H. RICHARD NIEBUHR: The Kingdom of God in America TB/49

RALPH BARTON PERRY: Puritanism and Democracy TB/1138

PAUL PFUETZE: Self, Society, Existence: *Human Nature and Dialogue in the Thought of George Herbert Mead and Martin Buber* TB/1059

WALTER RAUSCHENBUSCH: Christianity and the Social Crisis. ‡ *Edited by Robert D. Cross* TB/3059

KURT SAMUELSSON: Religion and Economic Action: *A Critique of Max Weber's* The Protestant Ethic and the Spirit of Capitalism. || ° *Trans. by E. G. French; Ed. with Intro. by D. C. Coleman* TB/1131

ERNST TROELTSCH: The Social Teaching of the Christian Churches ° Vol. I TB/71; Vol. II TB/72

NATURAL SCIENCES AND MATHEMATICS

Biological Sciences

CHARLOTTE AUERBACH: The Science of Genetics Σ TB/568

A. BELLAIRS: Reptiles: *Life History, Evolution, and Structure. Illus.* TB/520

LUDWIG VON BERTALANFFY: Modern Theories of Development: *An Introduction to Theoretical Biology* TB/554

LUDWIG VON BERTALANFFY: Problems of Life: *An Evaluation of Modern Biological and Scientific Thought* TB/521

HAROLD F. BLUM: Time's Arrow and Evolution TB/555

JOHN TYLER BONNER: The Ideas of Biology. Σ *Illus.* TB/570

A. J. CAIN: Animal Species and their Evolution. *Illus.* TB/519

WALTER B. CANNON: Bodily Changes in Pain, Hunger, Fear and Rage. *Illus.* TB/562

W. E. LE GROS CLARK: The Antecedents of Man: *An Introduction to the Evolution of the Primates.* ° *Illus.* TB/559

W. H. DOWDESWELL: Animal Ecology. *Illus.* TB/543

W. H. DOWDESWELL: The Mechanism of Evolution. *Illus.* TB/527

R. W. GERARD: Unresting Cells. *Illus.* TB/541

DAVID LACK: Darwin's Finches. *Illus.* TB/544

J. E. MORTON: Molluscs: *An Introduction to their Form and Functions. Illus.* TB/529

ADOLF PORTMANN: Animals as Social Beings. ° *Illus.* TB/572

O. W. RICHARDS: The Social Insects. *Illus.* TB/542

P. M. SHEPPARD: Natural Selection and Heredity. *Illus.* TB/528

EDMUND W. SINNOTT: Cell and Psyche: *The Biology of Purpose* TB/546

C. H. WADDINGTON: How Animals Develop. *Illus.* TB/553

Chemistry

J. R. PARTINGTON: A Short History of Chemistry. *Illus.* TB/522

J. READ: A Direct Entry to Organic Chemistry. *Illus.* TB/523

J. READ: Through Alchemy to Chemistry. *Illus.* TB/561

Communication Theory

J. R. PIERCE: Symbols, Signals and Noise: *The Nature and Process of Communication* TB/574

Geography

R. E. COKER: This Great and Wide Sea: *An Introduction to Oceanography and Marine Biology. Illus.* TB/551

F. K. HARE: The Restless Atmosphere TB/560

History of Science

W. DAMPIER, Ed.: Readings in the Literature of Science. *Illus.* TB/512

A. HUNTER DUPREE: Science in the Federal Government: *A History of Policies and Activities to 1940* TB/573

ALEXANDRE KOYRÉ: From the Closed World to the Infinite Universe: *Copernicus, Kepler, Galileo, Newton, etc.* TB/31

A. G. VAN MELSEN: From Atomos to Atom: *A History of the Concept* Atom TB/517

O. NEUGEBAUER: The Exact Sciences in Antiquity TB/552

H. T. PLEDGE: Science Since 1500: *A Short History of Mathematics, Physics, Chemistry and Biology. Illus.* TB/506

HANS THIRRING: Energy for Man: *From Windmills to Nuclear Power* TB/556

WILLIAM LAW WHYTE: Essay on Atomism: *From Democritus to 1960* TB/565

A. WOLF: A History of Science, Technology and Philosophy in the 16th and 17th Centuries. ° *Illus.* Vol. I TB/508; Vol. II TB/509

A. WOLF: A History of Science, Technology, and Philosophy in the Eighteenth Century. ° *Illus.* Vol. I TB/539; Vol. II TB/540

Mathematics

H. DAVENPORT: The Higher Arithmetic: *An Introduction to the Theory of Numbers* TB/526

H. G. FORDER: Geometry: *An Introduction* TB/548

GOTTLOB FREGE: The Foundations of Arithmetic: *A Logico-Mathematical Enquiry* TB/534

S. KÖRNER: The Philosophy of Mathematics: *An Introduction* TB/547

D. E. LITTLEWOOD: Skeleton Key of Mathematics: *A Simple Account of Complex Algebraic Problems* TB/525

GEORGE E. OWEN: Fundamentals of Scientific Mathematics TB/569

WILLARD VAN ORMAN QUINE: Mathematical Logic TB/558

O. G. SUTTON: Mathematics in Action. ° *Foreword by James R. Newman. Illus.* TB/518

FREDERICK WAISMANN: Introduction to Mathematical Thinking. *Foreword by Karl Menger* TB/511

Philosophy of Science

R. B. BRAITHWAITE: Scientific Explanation TB/515

J. BRONOWSKI: Science and Human Values. *Revised and Enlarged Edition* TB/505

ALBERT EINSTEIN et al.: Albert Einstein: Philosopher-Scientist. *Edited by Paul A. Schilpp* Vol. I TB/502 Vol. II TB/503

WERNER HEISENBERG: Physics and Philosophy: *The Revolution in Modern Science* TB/549

JOHN MAYNARD KEYNES: A Treatise on Probability. ° *Introduction by N. R. Hanson* TB/557

KARL R. POPPER: The Logic of Scientific Discovery TB/576

STEPHEN TOULMIN: Foresight and Understanding: *An Enquiry into the Aims of Science. Foreword by Jacques Barzun* TB/564

STEPHEN TOULMIN: The Philosophy of Science: *An Introduction* TB/513

G. J. WHITROW: The Natural Philosophy of Time ° TB/563

Physics and Cosmology

DAVID BOHM: Causality and Chance in Modern Physics. *Foreword by Louis de Broglie* TB/536

P. W. BRIDGMAN: The Nature of Thermodynamics TB/537

P. W. BRIDGMAN: A Sophisticate's Primer of Relativity TB/575

A. C. CROMBIE, Ed.: Turning Point in Physics TB/535

C. V. DURELL: Readable Relativity. *Foreword by Freeman J. Dyson* TB/530

ARTHUR EDDINGTON: Space, Time and Gravitation: *An outline of the General Relativity Theory* TB/510

GEORGE GAMOW: Biography of Physics Σ TB/567

MAX JAMMER: Concepts of Force: *A Study in the Foundation of Dynamics* TB/550

MAX JAMMER: Concepts of Mass *in Classical and Modern Physics* TB/571

MAX JAMMER: Concepts of Space: *The History of Theories of Space in Physics. Foreword by Albert Einstein* TB/533

EDMUND WHITTAKER: History of the Theories of Aether and Electricity
Volume I: *The Classical Theories* TB/531
Volume II: *The Modern Theories* TB/532

G. J. WHITROW: The Structure and Evolution of the Universe: *An Introduction to Cosmology. Illus.* TB/504

Code to Torchbook Libraries:

TB/1+	: The Cloister Library
TB/301+	: The Cathedral Library
TB/501+	: The Science Library
TB/1001+	: The Academy Library
TB/2001+	: The Bollingen Library
TB/3001+	: The University Library

A LETTER TO THE READER

Overseas, there is considerable belief that we are a country of extreme conservatism and that we cannot accommodate to social change.

Books about America in the hands of readers abroad can help change those ideas.

The U. S. Information Agency cannot, by itself, meet the vast need for books about the United States.

You can help.

Harper Torchbooks provides three packets of books on American history, economics, sociology, literature and politics to help meet the need.

To send a packet of Torchbooks [*] overseas, all you need do is send your check for $7 (which includes cost of shipping) to Harper & Row. The U. S. Information Agency will distribute the books to libraries, schools, and other centers all over the world.

I ask every American to support this program, part of a worldwide BOOKS USA campaign.

I ask you to share in the opportunity to help tell others about America.

EDWARD R. MURROW
Director,
U. S. Information Agency

[*retailing at $10.85 to $12.00]